ASSESSMENT AND DEVELOPMENT IN EUROPE

Latest titles in the McGraw-Hill Training Series

PRACTICAL INSTRUCTIONAL DESIGN FOR OPEN LEARNING
MATERIALS
A Modular Course Covering Open Learning, Computer Based Training and Multi-media
Nigel Harrison   ISBN 0-07-709055-1
DELIVERING 'IN-HOUSE' OUTPLACEMENT
A Practical Guide for Trainers, Managers and Personnel Specialists
Alan Jones   ISBN 0-07-707895-0
FACILITATION
Providing Opportunities For Learning
Trevor Bentley   ISBN 0-07-707684-2
DEVELOPMENT CENTRES
Realizing the Potential of Your Employees Through Assessment and Development
Geoff Lee and David Beard   ISBN 0-07-707785-7
DEVELOPING DIRECTORS
Building An Effective Boardroom Team
Colin Coulson-Thomas   ISBN 0-07-707590-0
MANAGING THE TRAINING PROCESS
Putting the Basics into Practice
Mike Wills   ISBN 0-07-707806-3
RESOURCE-BASED LEARNING
Using Open and Flexible Resources for Continuous Development
Julie Dorrell   ISBN 0-07-707692-3
WORKSHOPS THAT WORK
100 Ideas to Make Your Training Events More Effective
Tom Bourner, Vivien Martin, Phil Race   ISBN 0-07-707800-4
THE HANDBOOK FOR ORGANIZATIONAL CHANGE
Strategy and Skill for Trainers and Developers
Carol A. O'Connor   ISBN 0-07-707693-1
TRAINING FOR PROFIT
A Guide to the Integration of Training in an Organization's Success
Philip Darling   ISBN 0-07-707786-5
TEAM BUILDING
A Practical Guide for Trainers
Neil Clark   ISBN 0-07-707846-2
DEVELOPING MANAGERS AS COACHES
A Trainer's Guide
Frank Salisbury   ISBN 0-07-707892-6
THE ASSERTIVE TRAINER
A Practical Guide for Trainers
Liz Willis and Jenny Daisley   ISBN 0-07-707077-2
LEARNING TO CHANGE
A Resource for Trainers, Managers and Learners Based on Self-organized Learning
Sheila Harri-Augstein and Ian M. Webb   ISBN 0-07-707896-9

Details of these and other titles in the series are available from:

The Product Manager, Professional Books, McGraw-Hill Book Company Europe,
Shoppenhangers Road, Maidenhead, Berkshire SL6 2QL, United Kingdom
Tel: 01628 23432 Fax: 01628 770224

Assessment and development in Europe

Adding value to individuals and organizations

Mac Bolton, with Robert Bols, Victor Ernoult, Jan Gijswijt, Ulrike Hess, Hélio Moreira, Jean-Luc Spriet, Lou Van Beirendonck and Jos van Bree

McGRAW-HILL BOOK COMPANY

London · New York · St Louis · San Francisco · Auckland
Bogotá · Caracas · Lisbon · Madrid · Mexico · Milan
Montreal · New Delhi · Panama · Paris · San Juan · São Paulo
Singapore · Sydney · Tokyo · Toronto

Published by
McGRAW-HILL Book Company Europe
Shoppenhangers Road, Maidenhead, Berkshire, SL6 2QL, England
Telephone: 01628 23432
Fax: 01628 770224

British Library Cataloguing in Publication Data
Bolton, Mac
    Assessment and Development in Europe:
    Adding Value to Individuals and
    Organisations. – (McGraw-Hill Training
    Series)
    I. Title II. Series
    330.94

    ISBN 0-07-707928-0

12345 CUP 98765

Typeset by BookEns Limited, Baldock, Herts.
and printed and bound in Great Britain at the University Press, Cambridge

Printed on permanent paper in compliance with the ISO Standard 9706

We wish to dedicate this book to those who had the vision to create the European Union of nations, giving us the extra motivation to work together with unity of purpose.

Contents

Series preface

Training and development are now firmly centre stage in most organizations, if not all. Nothing unusual in that—for some organizations. They have always seen training and development as part of the heart of their businesses—but more and more must see it that same way.

The demographic trends through the 1990s will inject into the marketplace severe competition for good people who will need good training. Young people without conventional qualifications, skilled workers in redundant crafts, people out of work, women wishing to return to work—all will require excellent training to fit them to meet the job demands of the 1990s and beyond.

But excellent training does not spring from what we have done well in the past. T&D specialists are in a new ball game. 'Maintenance' training—training to keep up skill levels to do what we have always done—will be less in demand. Rather, organization, work and market change training are now much more important and will remain so for some time. Changing organizations and people is no easy task, requiring special skills and expertise which, sadly, many T&D specialists do not possess.

To work as a 'change' specialist requires us to get to centre stage—to the heart of the company's business. This means we have to ask about future goals and strategies, and even be involved in their development, at least as far as T&D policies are concerned.

This demands excellent communication skills, political expertise, negotiating ability, diagnostic skills—indeed, all the skills a good internal consultant requires.

The implications for T&D specialists are considerable. It is not enough merely to be skilled in the basics of training, we must also begin to act like business people and to think in business terms and talk the language of business. We must be able to resource training not just from within but by using the vast array of external resources. We must be able to manage our activities as well as any other manager. We must share in the creation and communication of the company's vision. We must never let the goals of the company out of our sight.

In short, we may have to grow and change with the business. It will be hard. We shall have to demonstrate not only relevance but also value for money and achievement of results. We shall be our own boss, as accountable for results as any other line manager, and we shall have to deal with fewer internal resources.

The challenge is on, as many T&D specialists have demonstrated to me over the past few years. We need to be capable of meeting that challenge. This is why McGraw-Hill Book Company Europe have planned and launched this major new training series—to help us meet that challenge.

The series covers all aspects of T&D and provides the knowledge base from which we can develop plans to meet the challenge. They are practical books for the professional person. They are a starting point for planning our journey into the twenty-first century.

Use them well. Don't just read them. Highlight key ideas, thoughts, action pointers or whatever, and have a go at doing something with them. Through experimentation we evolve; through stagnation we die.

I know that all the authors in the McGraw-Hill Training Series would want me to wish you good luck. Have a great journey into the twenty-first century.

ROGER BENNETT
Series Editor

About the series editor

Roger Bennett has over 20 years' experience in training, management education, research and consulting. He has long been involved with trainer training and trainer effectiveness. He has carried out research into trainer effectiveness, and conducted workshops, seminars, and conferences on the subject around the world. He has written extensively on the subject including the book *Improving Trainer Effectiveness*, Gower. His work has taken him all over the world and has involved directors of companies as well as managers and trainers.

Dr Bennett has worked in engineering, several business schools (including the International Management Centre, where he launched the UK's first masters degree in T&D), and has been a board director of two companies. He is the editor of the *Journal of European Industrial Training* and was series editor of the ITD's *Get In There* workbook and video package for the managers of training departments. He now runs his own business called The Management Development Consultancy.

About the contributors

Mac Bolton has been working in assessment and development for 30 years, mostly at Roffey Park Management Institute in West Sussex in Britain where he has been a tutor, consultant and researcher in the human area of management, specializing in work relating to assessment/development centres. As a founder member of Assessment Circle Europe he has cooperated with other members on projects in Holland and Portugal. Although not a linguist he learned about living and working in other cultures through spending five years in Uganda early in his career.

Mac started his working life in engineering in the North of England, gained a degree in Mechanical Sciences at Cambridge and later in his career trained in the Social Sciences culminating in a research degree in Social Psychology at the University of Sussex. He is a chartered psychologist and has written articles and booklets on several assessment and development topics.

Robert Bols has a degree in Psychology from the Catholic University of Louvain. After two years' experience in a middle management position in an international service company he first worked as an independent trainer and later as a consultant specializing in the assessment centre method.

He was a member of the organizing committee of the Third European Congress on the Assessment Centre Method and set up, together with Lou Van Beirendonck, the Belgian Congress on the Assessment Centre Method, held for the third time in 1994.

He joined Quintessence two yeas ago where he is working in the area of the setting up and operation of assessment and development centres and the implementation of the assessment centre method and other criterion-based appraisal systems in organizations. He has spoken on this subject at several national and international congresses and workshops.

Victor Ernoult has a degree from the Higher School of Applied Psychology in France where he is now a Professor while also being a consultant. He founded and is President of Infraplan Ernoult Search, a direct search executive company and human resources consulting firm in Paris, which includes assessment centre methods among its skills, and he is now also President of Optimhom, the daughter company of Infraplan, which specializes in assessment centre approaches.

For several years Victor directed the Recruitment and Career Development Division of Rank Xerox in France and he has also worked at the United Nations in New York. He has an M.A. from the University of New York. He has carried out numerous international assignments in the USA and in South East Asia in particular, and has had two books published on human resource matters as well as several articles.

Jan Gijswijt has a degree in Social Psychology from the University of Amsterdam and spent much of his working life building up a human resource development institute in Holland, Gijswijt Trainingen. As a founder of Vetron, the Dutch association of training and development institutes, he played a central role in the professionalization of training and development in the Netherlands. He also worked in adult education at Michigan State University in the USA, but returned to his native Holland with a French wife, Magali Noël. He speaks French, Dutch, German and English and by this means was a key initiator of the cross-Europe contacts that formed Assessment Circle Europe.

Although no longer actively involved in Gijswijt Trainingen, now Gijswijt Organisatie & Ontwikkeling, he is interested in facilitating the international work of Assessment Circle Europe and has also developed links with Poland.

Ulrike Hess is a founder partner of tpm (Team für Psychologisches Management), established at Bubenreuth in North Bavaria, Germany in 1969, which provides the German representation in Assessment Circle Europe. She has a Dipl.-Psychologe from the University of Erlangen-Nuremburg where she has also been an assistant professor.

With tpm, Ulrike has been active in consultancy work with leading German companies, designing and running assessment centres and development programmes that in recent years have extended to Austria, Turkey, Hungary, former East Germany and Poland. Her work has been published in books and she has presented papers at conferences of applied psychologists.

Hélio Moreira is managing partner of ADQ Management Consultants, a company which is part of the EGOR Portugal Group which he helped to found in 1986 as a part of the international Egor Group. As a psychologist he is experienced in human resources consultancy and is a leading practitioner in the use of assessment centre methods in Portugal. His main interest is concentrated in change and helping companies to adapt to new business environments.

Hélio's consultancy team is active in management selection and development, team planning, marketing, strategy and organization.

Jean-Luc Spriet is Associate Director and Partner of Optimhom Le Bilan Comportemental, a daughter company of Infraplan, based in Paris. He has had management responsibilities in various companies and also set up the first French outplacement counselling office.

Jean-Luc has an MBA from Ecole Supérieure de Commerce de Paris and has designed and operated a large number of assessment centres for companies in different professional environments. He also trains managers in recruitment and assessment.

Lou Van Beirendonck has a degree in Industrial Psychology from the University of Leuven; he also has a degree in Organizational Development and an MBA

Lou started his career with Ford Werke, where he carried out an investigation on quality circles. Later he started working as a consultant and founded Quintessence, a consulting firm with offices in Antwerp and Brussels. He is also Professor on the Management School IPO in Antwerp and contributes to the Human Resources Management course of the Ehsal Management School in Brussels.

Quintessence is known in Belgium as a leading institute for assessment centres. Training and development activities also form an important part of their business. In 1994, Quintessence consisted of a team of 10 professionals, all working in the field of assessment and development.

Jos van Bree is one of the founders of Interselling Groep and director of Interselect and Optimum selectie adviesgroep. He has a degree in business administration. Under his direction selection instruments relating to assessment/development centres were developed and applied for recruitment and selection, interview techniques and capacity tests. In Holland both Interselect and Optimum selectie adviesgroep are leading organizations in assessment centres. Working with professionals gives them the advantage of being able to develop tailor-made assessment centres for various purposes.

Optimum is (together with Gijswijt) the Dutch representative in Assessment Circle Europe.

Preface
Mac Bolton

Events in Europe are moving fast. Not only is the European Union attempting to bring together different systems and approaches on a tight timetable, but other countries from the former Eastern European group are becoming increasingly involved. How do we assess and use the differing abilities and cultures? Is it best to try to bring them into a common framework of abilities, or is it better to value the differences and seek to match abilities to the cultural strengths of the local situation?

After grappling with these kinds of issues for a few years, we (the authors), who are all members of a cross-national group called Assessment Circle Europe (ACE), find that there is no one solution to these and related problems. Each project or human resource need can demand a unique solution dependent on what kind of company, whether national, international or cross-national, is involved. The level of role, managerial or not, and the degree of expectation of progression to other roles, will determine some part of the answer. Certainly we have found that the 'standard package' is to be avoided as assessment and development methods are designed for each situation. The kind of challenge being faced in our work can be illustrated by the following projects:

- an international company setting up a new factory in Portugal and deciding how to put together a local and international team
- a Scandinavian-owned British company seeking to identify and develop future senior managers to meet the requirements of the group throughout the world
- a manufacturing facility being put together in former East Germany with management and operations conforming to West German and international standards.

Although there cannot be a standard solution to these situations it may be helpful at this early stage of the book to outline some broad principles of the process to be engaged in to ensure that the projects are successful. The aim is to equip the managers and staff of the organizations to add extra value to their operations by reliable, valid assessment of the potential of the people and suitable training and development to fulfil that potential. Whatever the technological sophistication of the equipment or the size of financial investment, the expertise of the people will be crucial for obtaining the full value of the investment and the equipment. With changing needs people may indeed be able to add value to an existing investment.

So the broad principles of the process are likely to be :

- a full diagnosis of the wider context, cultural background and the actual content of the jobs, roles and careers that will be needed by the organization that is planning ahead
- a clear specification, in language that expresses the necessary behaviour, of the abilities needed to perform the roles that will be required
- methods of assessment that determine how far people have the potential, or are already competent, to perform those roles
- an approach to development that will stimulate and support the attainment of full competence in the actual situations in which the people work and encourage continuing development as new needs emerge
- a means of evaluating the success of the process of assessment and development, including detecting the need for changes and modification in approach.

It is rare to find that all five of these principles are carried out effectively in any one organization or project, and we ourselves make no claim of perfection. Full implementation depends on many factors, some of which may be difficult to control in the fast-changing economic, political and social environment in which we are working in Europe. This, however, is no excuse for not attempting to carry out the process in an informed, systematic way. Standards have been set, and in each country there are some aspects that are notably thorough and worth recording for others to use as a stimulus for their own work. We have learned from each other's strengths and used such ideas, suitably modified, to improve methods used in other situations. A joint workshop was held in 1990 in The Netherlands to which a variety of people from organizations in nine countries came to share and learn from each other about assessment and development methods.

Cooperation and learning have progressed through other meetings, joint projects and studies. This book attempts to capture some of the significant parts of this work on a cross-national basis. It is written to share with our readers the experience and insights which may help when companies attempt to assess and develop people in a country that is not familiar to them or for cross-national roles. The assumption is that performance will be improved by suitable systematic and valid methods which will also give increased job satisfaction and opportunity for development. Some chapters report the sum (or difference) of the approaches used in a number of countries, while others show how cross-cultural factors need to be carefully considered within a project.

In Chapter 1 we point out some of the historical influences behind assessment and development of people in work organizations, contrasting those influences in different countries. Drawing particularly on experience in working in both Britain and Portugal the authors trace the different backgrounds in theory and practice which have, by separate routes, led to the growth of interest in the assessment centre method, and also with that to some pioneering work in systems of performance improvement and career development. From this, some limitations in these methods are noted as well as the advantages, and some of the principles for success are outlined, recognizing that they cannot be applied regardless of circumstances, culture or country. Right away we need to make clear that we see assessment and development as linked processes in that where there is potential ability it needs careful nurturing and stimulating in order to be turned into realized performance. We see no clear distinction, for instance, between assessment centres and development centres, but rather a continuum where assumptions, methods and responsibilities need to be clearly defined so that individuals and organizations are in no doubt about who is doing what at each stage of the process.

In Chapter 2 we go into some detail about three cases in different countries of Europe as practical examples of assessment and development schemes which are true to their respective contexts. This may help to meet the need of some readers to be able to see the practical detail of setting up schemes where there are the commercial pressures of quality standards, meeting deadlines, having limited resources and involving line managers in the key processes of assessing and developing people. Although there are differences in approach in the three cases, because of the special needs of the businesses concerned, some common elements are identified to link the cases together indicating the potential of looking cross-nationally to achieve the added value from the situations.

Then in Chapter 3 we attempt to show how any scheme of assessment and development such as those described in Chapter 2 needs to fit within a total strategy for human resource development. We have the benefit, too, in that chapter of Victor Ernoult's insights into French ways of thinking in linking the applications of any strategy with theoretical considerations in human resource management. The special challenges are shown of introducing a new method, such as assessment centres, into organizations whose management style, as seen in the line managers, has cultural 'givens' which contradict the assumptions of the new method. Managers whose eyesight is limited to what they have seen in the local situation provide conditions which are not favourable to a wider strategy. The European market makes it important to consider any project or scheme for assessment and development within a wide planning context and to avoid taking a narrow approach using a limited source or method for developing the human resources needed. This leads on to the contrasting theme in Chapter 4 where differences within the various parts of Europe are identified, some of them apparently not easily reconcilable without detailed psychological and social changes. The implications for projects involving cross-cultural assessment are drawn out from the three studies.

It has become clear in carrying out assessment work in the changing conditions of the nineties that it is not enough to predict the potential which people have: considerable attention and support needs to be given to realizing that potential. Chapter 5 shows how some of that support can be planned in a strategic framework and then applied by ensuring that there is maximum commitment from all directions. An increasingly close link between assessment and development is seen as vital if strategic change is to be achieved. The integration of methods from different countries has been shown to be useful when facing a necessary change of culture in order that the full benefit of the initiative is obtained. A case in Portugal that drew on experience in other countries, especially Britain, where privatization and the accompanying culture change had already been experienced, shows the need for highly supportive development programmes linked to assessment for placement of managers in new posts. From Belgium we also learn that there are limits to the development that is possible in some areas of performance—the concept of trainability raised in that chapter in relation to assessment for development seems to be breaking new ground.

Then in Chapter 6 we attempt to point out the emerging issues and some of the unanswered questions in taking a longer-term European view of assessment and development. The use of computer-based methods to improve the reliability and effectiveness of assessment and placement of staff shows promise. The early identification of potential, combined with obtaining views of staff about working cross-nationally, can be an important part of building up a source of future international managers. This may also be linked with the growing emphasis on encouraging self-assessment and self-development for the changing opportunities. One of the most challenging issues, particularly as Europe widens to include new language groups in non-EU countries, is to be able to carry out cross-national assessments either in local languages or in the business language of an international company. Two projects are reported on in Chapter 7 which show how this challenge was faced and overcome, needing considerable care and effort. The need for fairness and being reliable in identifying potential require increased sensitivity to sources of cultural and language disadvantage which adds to the longer-standing issues of discrimination on the basis of gender and ethnic origin. Recent conflicts have shown that Europe has limited ability as yet to apply assessment and opportunities for development in an objective way for all communities within the continent. Whatever progress the authors have made is only a beginning in the challenging task ahead of us all.

Finally in Chapter 8 we report on our attempt to work together across borders in researching the key skills needed in managers who are aiming to have cross-national careers. We are optimistic that a new generation of managers can be developed who will be skilled in the behaviours represented by the criteria which we have identified. Our work together has helped us to be more sensitive to these skills and we can vouch for the fact that it has been an enjoyable experience as we have learned from each other. The following pages should convey some of the flavour of that experience.

Acknowledgements

This book has depended on the goodwill, comments and cooperation of a considerable number of people in many countries. Colleagues and clients of all the authors include people in many countries of Europe and a few beyond. There are too many to list them all here, and there would be a danger of omitting some if we tried.

We have used research results reported by Rui Ribeiro in Chapter 1 and we are grateful for his permission to reproduce these. We use data from Ericsson Limited in Chapter 4, coupled with the company name, so we gladly acknowledge their helpfulness in giving us permission to do so. Also in relation to Chapter 4, we wish to thank Mr Guy Truong, Director of Human Resources of SOREFI, Poitou-Charentes, who evaluated the assessment project for Caisses d'Epargne Ecureuil in France, and we thank Mrs Magali Noël, a specialist in French civilization and intercultural relations at the University of Amsterdam, who gave her valuable and much appreciated comments on some cultural aspects.

As might be expected, we are greatly indebted to the expertise and support of translators, secretaries and those who do marvels with word processors and software packages. As editor (senior author and co-ordinator), I will use my privileged position to mention Valerie Garrow, Sandra Fonseca, Jennie Johnson and Ann Emerson for their most helpful contributions.

In Portugal, family relationships are valued highly and I therefore feel it is right to allow Hélio Moreira (in recognition of the support which all the authors have received from their families) to represent us all in expressing gratitude to all the families. He thanks his wife, Maria Antónia, for her support, criticisms and availability, and his children, Nuno and Tiago, for sacrificing their weekends.

Finally we are most appreciative of the way that the editors at McGraw-Hill Book Company Europe have had faith in our ability to make the European concept work—cooperating effectively as partners in a European community of fellow-workers and authors.

Mac Bolton

1 Assessing and developing people: the background

Mac Bolton and Hélio Moreira

In this chapter we sketch some of the historical influences in different parts of Europe which provide the framework for the issues, case studies and theoretical stances which are opened up in more detail in later chapters. We see how assessment and development have gradually come together in Britain and in a much shorter time scale in Portugal, illustrating the range of experience of many of the countries of the European Union.

Assessing people for roles and careers

What is the best method of assessing people for work roles? This question, like a similar one on the best method of developing people which we will be facing later, seems an obvious one to ask whenever there is a need to find, promote or develop people suited to roles in an organization. Studies and observation of managers do not suggest that this question is very often asked in a radical way. Each organization (and each country) has its favoured method or methods which tend to be carried through into a new human resource need without the question being asked 'Is it the best method?' For instance, the panel interview has been used for many years in local government organizations in Britain, graphology has had its advocates in France and testing has been used for some years by organizations in Portugal.

It does not need an advanced education in psychology to realize that each role or career may have special demands which need to be assessed by methods that reliably predict the potential of people. These methods will depend on the nature of the ability involved. So a process of simple logical reasoning leads one to the question 'What method is best for predicting any defined ability?' The conclusion that follows is that each ability could need a different method, and careful design will be required to ensure valid assessments of people. For instance, a systems analyst may need to be able to carry out logical analysis in considerable depth, a sales assistant in a department store will need to be able to establish relationships with customers quickly and easily, and a bridge construction worker will need a good head for heights, among other qualities. The methods of assessment of these abilities will be different if reliable results are to be obtained. A reasoning test is unlikely to be appropriate for the second and third examples although it may suit the first example. Taking people up to a great height would be a waste of time (and possibly dangerous!) for the first and second examples.

It may be helpful here to list the variety of methods that are in general use, from which a suitable mix can be drawn to suit a defined need:

1 Application forms and other written evidence asked for from candidates
2 References and reports on the candidates from defined people, e.g. supervisors of the candidates
3 Interviews (one-to-one or panel)
4 Tests of ability or personality
5 Situational exercises.

Historical influences on assessment

Interest in applying more systematic methods to assessment took a step forward following on from the First World War. In Britain the National Institute of Industrial Psychology was founded in London in 1921 (although it was wound up in 1977 when its work passed on to others) and with the enthusiasm initially of Charles Myers pioneered methods of job analysis, interview training and the use of testing. A similar body was set up in France in 1928, with support from government funds. The British work influenced the thinking of personnel and training staff over those 56 years, and there are many who still remember the framework for personnel specification, devised by Alec Rodger in 1930, known as the Seven Point Plan. This provided a basic classification of human characteristics which enabled assessors to be more systematic and thorough in investigation and decision making. The seven headings were:

1 Physical make-up
2 Attainments
3 General intelligence
4 Special aptitudes
5 Interests
6 Disposition
7 Circumstances.

It is less well known that Ken Rawling was invited, after Alec Rodger's death, to do a revision of this plan to take account of recent developments in psychology. This new booklet, which also includes Rodger's original booklet (Rawling, 1985), gives a reformulation of the characteristics, with full explanation of their components, into six identifiable areas forming a total dynamic model of an individual:

1 Physical characteristics

2 Attainments
3 Abilities
4 Motivation
5 Personality
6 Circumstances.

The terms used are more in tune with current usage of assessment instruments, e.g. ability tests and personality questionnaires, and with behavioural descriptions used in defining various forms of motivation. What these schemes do not take account of so well is the increased emphasis on behavioural *outputs* in performance such as are defined in schemes of 'competences' or in the criteria at the heart of the design of assessment centres, as illustrated in Chapter 2. Nevertheless, in the early work in Britain strong emphasis was placed on job analysis as a basis for assessment and career development. This history has given a background to theory and practice which differs from some other countries in Europe. There are differences *within* countries as well as *between* countries in the range of methods used. For instance, in Britain references are not regarded as reliable in much of the private business sector, whereas in the public sector they are taken seriously. Between countries a major difference in the use of situational exercises is seen, as measured by the extent of use of the assessment centre method. In Britain (and to a lesser extent in Germany) the Second World War caused new methods of selection of forces personnel to be sought and situational exercises were used. This was carried forward in Britain after the war to the Civil Service Selection Board, as described by one of the psychologists involved (Anstey, 1989 and 1977). Some business organizations used group exercises in the fifties and sixties, but the assessment centre method as developed in the USA (Thornton and Byham, 1982) began to be used in Britain more widely in the seventies, combining British approaches with American research and experience, as in AT&T and IBM (Stewart and Stewart, 1981).

This contrasts with the picture in France where there was little to report about situational exercises before 1980 (Ernoult, Gruère and Pezeu, 1984) and assessment centres are still relatively unknown in most French organizations. The interview is still the most popular method there and, for managerial posts, applicants normally experience several interviews with different people (Shackleton and Newell, 1993), with less reliance being placed on references than in some other countries. The use of graphology (handwriting analysis) is quite extensive, with a majority of large private sector companies in France making some use of this method, which is rarely used in other countries except for French-speaking Belgium.

In Holland the first traces of assessment centres can be found shortly after the Second World War when the Dutch army urgently needed many officers for its expeditionary forces for the final campaign against Japan and the liberation of Indonesia. AKZO, formerly AKU, also experimented with assessment centres during the fifties; however, it took two more decades before they became more generally known. At the end of the seventies Mars became one of the most widely known—and quoted—companies where assessment centres were used for selection and for human resource development. Since the eighties the method has penetrated steadily, starting with the bigger, mainly internationally orientated companies but also becoming increasingly evident in government organizations and state companies such as PTT, (the Post Office) and NS (Dutch Railways) and, last but not least, in Dutch banking companies.

As continuing education always plays an important part in the educational scene in Holland and part-time MBA training has boomed recently throughout the country, assessment centres have found quite wide application as part of the admission procedures and have become familiar to most people in key positions. We can now observe the growing application of derived instruments such as applications of situational assessment not only in selection and admission procedures but also in appraisal and training exercises. The traditional 'Johari window' feedback exercise, for instance, is no longer linked to the usual subjective evaluation but to systematized assessments.

Recently we have observed in Holland an increased use of assessment centres in outplacement procedures and of development centres with the accent on career development for reorientation or for stimulating mobility.

In Germany over the last 10 to 15 years use of the assessment centre procedure has increased, and it is now used in almost all major companies as well as in the public service sector. It is more often used to select external applicants rather than to evaluate the potential of the company's own employees for personnel training and development. The quality of the procedures differs greatly. Often interviews together with a test or a questionnaire are called assessment centres. The concept of fairness and transparency to participants is often not given as much attention as it should be, therefore the image of this procedure is not always perceived as a positive one. A number of books on the subject of assessment centres have now been published and offer help to future participants in preparing themselves for an assessment centre.

Belgium somewhat follows the evolution of Holland and Germany, but a bit later. Over the last six years assessment centres have become a widespread selection tool, but this does not mean that former selection methods are regarded as old-fashioned or less valuable. Belgian companies and, since Brussels has become the headquarters of the European Union, many head offices or coordination centres of multinational organizations consider the assessment centre method as an *extra* tool, 'another opinion', but one that is essential, in screening a person. The Dutch-speaking part of Belgium is particularly fond of the objective results that emerge from such an evaluation. It is crucial to many human resource management people that a person's behaviour can be measurable and objectively observable.

Although the assessment centre is a fairly new method in Belgium it has spread very readily. One could say that in 1993 about 30 per cent of the bigger companies (banks as well as production plants) have made some use of assessment centres as a selection method and 5 per cent have fully implemented the method, not only as a selection instrument but also as a reliable overall human resources management tool.

Historical influences on assessment and development of people in Portugal

The assessment of human performance in Portugal has had a close relationship in the past to psychological tests. According to the results of a study (Almeida and Ribeiro, 1991) 85 per cent of the Portuguese psychologists who worked in companies, in an educational area or in clinical practice, resorted to this kind of instrument whenever they made their interventions, namely through the use of tests of intelligence and ability, projective techniques, personality questionnaires and sensory and psycho-motor assessments, especially in the case of equipment operators and drivers. Some consulting companies added to the results of tests some data gathered during group situations and interviews.

The public services, banks, insurance companies, telecommunication companies and consultants in recruitment and selection always used tests (largely because this had been negotiated with the trade unions) whenever they needed to examine someone to be placed, promoted or transferred to a functional area different from the one in which he or she already had experience. The kind of jobs for which tests were used rarely included senior or managerial positions; in this case references and analysis of the applicant's CV were more often put to use.

The army made a special contribution to the spread of the use of tests because all new recruits were asked to do these in order to assess their profiles of personal characteristics and guide them towards the different military branches. It is, however, also in the army that we can find the use of simulations in order to select potential sergeants and officers. This practice has been progressing along with the so-called 'situational tests'.

The results of these assessments were aimed mainly at aptitude diagnosis and comparison between individuals. Sometimes they served as career guidance. They were not usually a starting point for training nor did they involve very exhaustive validation studies.

The big public services organizations used to live under an atmosphere of protection provided by government regulations and by undemanding customers which allowed them to keep costs high and service levels below those offered by their European competitors. The management of companies was mainly characterized by an attitude of 'command and control' which left little space for innovation, quality and individual initiatives. Therefore the competence of staff was not a critical factor for business, and low levels of technical and behavioural competence were the consequential result of the fact that many managers did not expect much from their employees' contribution—if the contrary proved to be the case it was rarely seen as a company asset. Consequently assessment and training were given low priority, often being considered as a cost needed to maintain morale and not as investment in people which leads to a strong benefit or profit.

The present situation in Portugal

The entry of Portugal into the European Union, combined with an important increase in foreign investment, had as a consequence the import of more sophisticated practices of human resource management and the access of Portuguese customers to different goods and services which made them become more demanding. To these consequences there must also be added the recession of the last few years which struck our European partners and, perhaps in a more dramatic way, Portugal, because our starting point was worse: one of lower economic effectiveness. These facts caused companies to change in order to improve the quality of their services, capacity and efficiency.

Service companies were the first to try to reorganize themselves. In banks, computing and information services were the first to indicate that urgent changes were needed. In telecommunications, the first signs of change appeared in the commercial and sales areas; industry followed suit.

The majority of reorganization projects modified structures, size, relations between departments, and working procedures. Consequently new obligations and competences appeared and most companies did not have people qualified in these areas. New procedures had to be put in place. Companies have to search among their own workforce and through external recruitment to find people with the required new qualifications and necessary skills. Senior management are now able to understand that people will be the key factor in the process of reorganization, although they do not know how to recognize and develop the kind of people they need within a short space of time because companies have not had that experience.

It was in this context that in 1989 one of the biggest Portuguese banks, Banco Português do Atlantico, attempted to use a new assessment method, the assessment centre, and also opened the way to the development of a new type of practice in training—self-managed learning—for its computing and information systems office staff. In the last five years other companies have followed suit, among them Telecom Portugal and UBP (União de Bancos Portugueses).

The assessment of people in Portugal has seen a search take place for new techniques and working tools. And now we are using different methods as shown by a recent study (Ribeiro, 1993), presented during the first meeting of a group discussing organizational behaviour.

This study was based on the answers of about 20 companies drawn from a group of the 100 biggest national companies. The companies were presented with 12 assessment methods which included:

- tests: cognitive, sensory and psycho-motor ability
- self-descriptive questionnaires
- projective tests
- group exercises
- work samples
- assessment centres
- curriculum vitae
- references
- interviews
- graphology

and had to answer several questions, three of which are as follows.

Which methods are most used?　The distribution percentages of utilization of each of the methods suggest that those who wish to be selected face a probability of over 80 per cent of having to present their curriculum vitae or fill in a biographical questionnaire and of having an interview. Of the remaining methods covered by this study and shown in Figure 1.1, cognitive ability tests are most used, followed by self-descriptive questionnaires. It is important to notice that methodologies like assessment centres or work samples present low percentages of use in comparison to the remaining methods.

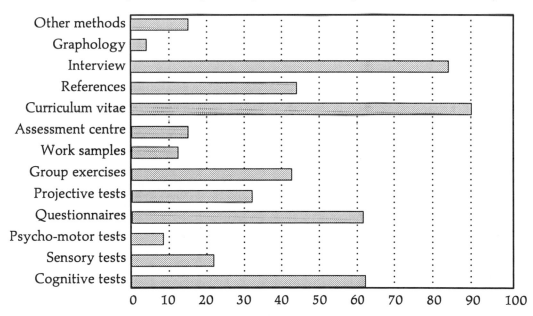

Figure 1.1　*Percentage of users*

Which methods are more valid?   In looking at Figure 1.2 it seems important to realize that from the total of 12 methods on which the companies were asked to give their opinions, seven present high values of perceived validity, with 50–70 per cent of the users considering them as more valid. We must underline the low score obtained by graphology and references. It is also important to mention here that some of the techniques included, such as assessment centres, are not so well known that everyone has a common understanding of the kind of practices and formal procedures which are involved. Therefore knowledge of a certain method and the results obtained depend on what has previously been experienced in a particular organization.

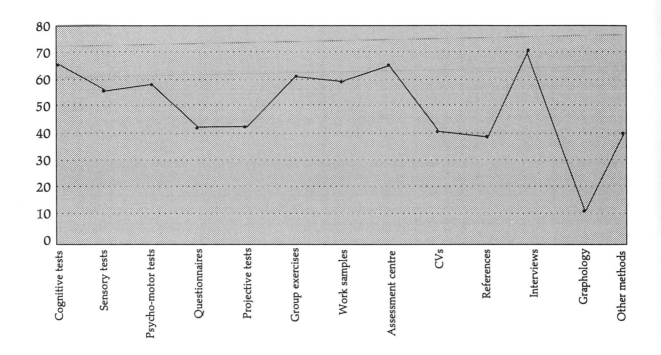

Figure 1.2   *The perceived validity of different methods*

Which is most important?   The answer to this question is clear: the assessment centre. As we can see in Figure 1.3, interviews appear in second place, with an average importance of 30 per cent.

Conclusion   In Portugal companies mostly use interviews, the analysis of curriculum vitae and cognitive ability tests as means of assessment. They consider assessment centres a very important method of assessment, but they see other methods as being equally valid.

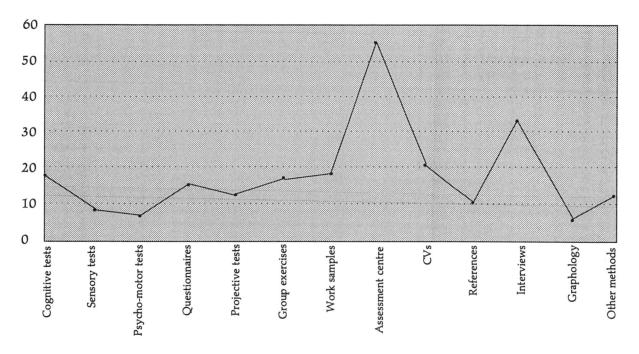

Figure 1.3 *Relative importance of different methods*

The future for assessment centres in Portugal

Assessment centres are already considered very important although, as yet, only a few companies have experimented with them and only a small number of these had the conditions to implement them properly in order to obtain their benefits. It is still not clear what possibilities they represent as tools not only of assessment but also of development and for implementing a new way of doing things. In the rapidly changing atmosphere which Portuguese companies are facing, the purposes for which people are being assessed keep being changed as business objectives are adapted to the changing economic environment. We face a time of experiment and search for new models which may provide us, in the shortest possible period of time, with a similar answer to that given by other European companies.

We think that companies have already realized that human resources are a key factor for success and it is possible to identify a trend towards greater valuing of the human factor in companies. This is why the study mentioned a high rank of importance given by the companies to assessment centres which we believe will be responsible for an increase in the number of users of this method.

Development in Britain and beyond

In some respects the full development of people has been an area of organizational behaviour which has been slow to blossom in Britain—certainly in comparison with the attention given to assessment. Even slower has been the making of a link between assessment and development which is one of the key themes of this book. Education and training of a largely formal kind has been valued by some industries, notably engineering, for more than 50 years, and schemes of apprenticeship, combined with college attendance, were available to a small part of the population.

Other countries of Europe, notably Germany, Holland and France have had systems of study that have taken young people through a development process that lasted longer than in Britain. For example, degree courses in Britain have largely lasted only three years, whereas other countries regard this as too short a period for full graduate status. Nevertheless, there may have been an advantage in this because it has long been recognized in Britain that further training and development is needed to be worthy of full professional status. Thus provision has been made for many years for post-graduate and other forms of training and development.

In a similar way to assessment, it was a world war that provided some stimulus in Britain for further development: this time it was the Second World War rather than the First. The government's Training Within Industry scheme was started to speed up the learning process so that people became skilled more quickly. It was in 1946 that Roffey Park Institute (now Roffey Park Management Institute) was set up, stimulated by some initiatives during the war that focused on the welfare and productiveness of people in industry. A few months later The Management College at Henley came into existence (then called The Administrative Staff College). Apprenticeship schemes spread, further education colleges widened their services and some companies set up their own training schemes for supervisors and managers, though this was largely confined to a few of the larger companies; smaller companies tended to feed off the supply of people trained by the larger companies.

Government intervention

Thus it was that pressure built up for legislation to try to ensure that every company of any size contributed to the development of skilled and trained people for each industry. The Industrial Training Act of 1964 set up Training Boards for the main industrial sectors and, although they operated through a somewhat mechanistic levy and grant system to reward companies that provided effective training, one effect of this intervention was to direct attention to training needs, methods of learning and the research that was needed to underpin better training. The Central Training Council Research Committee (and its successor, the Training Research Advisory Committee) sponsored research and the development of innovative methods to encourage more effective learning and development. One recipient of research grants was the Industrial Training Research Unit led by Eunice Belbin and Meredith Belbin; some of their findings began to challenge the assumption that formal teaching and training methods were effective in occupational learning and they pointed to the need for adaptation to ensure successful learning by adults and by young people who had little formal educational background (Belbin, 1969).

A modified form of government intervention resulted from a major review of training and of training facilities (Department of Employment, 1972) which included a comparison with France, Germany and Sweden. The case was made for more substantial investment in training facilities for individuals. The Manpower Services Commission and its agencies were set up as a result of the Employment and Training Act 1973, which amended the 1964 Act, and since 1988 these services have been replaced and largely decentralized to Training and Enterprise Councils in the regions. Through this history of government intervention considerable investment has been put into various forms of development, and yet consistency has been lacking as policies have changed from year to year.

In the management sector steady development has been seen since the setting up of the Foundation for Management Education in the sixties with government support. The London and Manchester Business Schools were founded and increasingly since then individuals have sought to gain an MBA through various forms of study, full-time and part-time, at business schools, universities and other institutions, through distance learning and self-managed learning, as a way of becoming professionally equipped for a management role. It is interesting that in Germany recognition of the value of an MBA has been slow to develop, perhaps because initial professional training is seen to be so thorough that further development is not considered necessary. However, there are signs now that individuals are not so satisfied and are taking part in programmes in other countries.

What is the best method of developing people?

In the brief historical outline above we have avoided defining some of the terms used in connection with development and have barely raised the question of how we can ensure that people learn the things that will be important to them in the future. It is time now to become more specific, but first it may help point to some of the issues if we list some of the crucial questions.

1 What is development?
2 How does development differ from training?
3 Is development related to individuals or is it linked with organizational changes?
4 Is formal training in groups still justifiable?
5 How do we ensure that people learn what they need in the immediate future?
6 How do we arrange that people 'learn how to learn' for the longer term?
7 Whose responsibility is it to learn, plan to learn, or manage the learning?

8 Do people all learn in the same kind of way in a specific situation?

9 What is the best method of developing people?

It would take many pages to attempt to answer all these questions and no doubt others that readers would like to add to the list. Some of the following chapters of this book, particularly Chapter 5, provide a few answers, but our view is that after nearly 50 years of post-war effort in improving our methods of doing business we are still amateurs in Europe at managing the learning and development process. Our aim in these rapidly changing times should surely be to ensure that all those involved in our business (or public service) are capable not only of surviving the demands but of flourishing and contributing the extra added value which will make a difference to the business and the world.

Parables have a long-standing record for conveying truth and understanding so here is a story, a true story, which may help to answer some of the questions listed above.

A parable   This is about a visit by two of the contributors to this book to the headquarters of a big international company located not far from the borders of three European countries. The problem presented to us, in English, was that the company had some very good training courses for its managers, but the managers themselves were not signing up to attend the courses. How could we help the company to achieve better attendance on these courses?

The visitors asked questions of the assembled group of training managers to discover some of the facts behind the situation. They then proposed that a first step would be to ask a representative group of managers to come together for part of a day to explore their needs for improving as managers to meet current business demands, and from that the training managers could begin to plan how these needs might best be met. An attempt was made to explain the difference between the concepts of 'teaching' and 'learning' only to be met with silence, eventually broken by one courteous training manager who explained that as they translated the words 'teaching' and 'learning' in their minds into their local language they ended up with the same word for both. This is perhaps indicative of the way in which, in many parts of Europe, we have inherited a view of learning that is teacher-dependent.

Our visit was not a great success as we had not given the company any help in ensuring that its managers attended the courses being provided. A year or so later it was reported to us that a new approach was beginning to appear—the need for the managers' participation in the planning and learning process had begun to be recognized.

Theory and practice   In many countries of Europe there is a long and proud tradition of education, in some cases based on the assumption that the teacher helps others to understand the theoretical concepts which have been abstracted from past experience, research and debate. This may not be the most helpful way of developing people who have not been altogether successful in the formal education system, and this is why the work of the Industrial Training Research Unit, mentioned above (Belbin, 1969) was important in reporting experiments that started from the experience, attitudes and capabilities for learning of the trainees themselves. One of the specific applications of the work of that Unit was in linking together assessment and training in the form of trainability testing (Downs, 1985), the essential characteristics of which are:

- it is job-based, job-specific and practical
- it has a structured learning period during which the candidate is encouraged to ask questions
- the trainer also acts as an assessor, using an error checklist, but only tests on what has been trained
- it incorporates the crucial aspects of the job and is validated against performance in training.

Occupations for which trainability tests have been devised are many and various, but include bricklayers, building society managers and dentists. The concept of trainability is further developed by Lou Van Beirendonck later in this book (second part of Chapter 5).

In the management development area, those who were pioneers in the field, such as Roffey Park, were strongly committed to the participative method of learning, recognizing that experienced managers would want to relate any theoretical ideas offered to them with the practical challenges of their managerial roles. It was only if these connections could be made that such people would value a week spent in an off-the-job situation. Modular approaches began to be seen as one way of bringing together theory and practice.

When the major business schools were launched in Britain from 1965 onwards, providing post-graduate degrees from established universities, it was inevitable that they would start by using the didactic methods of such universities, modified slightly by visiting fellows from Harvard Business School and other institutes with long experience of running MBA programmes.

One person who had doubts about this approach to developing management education was Reg Revans, who then had a lecturing appointment at Manchester University. He reacted to the plans by moving to Belgium to become Managing Director of the Inter-University Program, affiliated with the Foundation Industrie-Université of Brussels, which was launched in March 1968. Although there was tutorial work, assisted by reading and written exercises, the main feature of the formal learning was a full-time field study, lasting eight months, of a policy problem in an enterprise *other than the participant's own.*

The essential idea was that participants would be involved in *actions* in an environment where they would need to learn fast and that they would also draw on the expertise of tutors, fellow-participants and a group of business school professors in the USA who were linked with them. They received support and challenge at appropriate times as they put their proposals into effect, and they were expected to reflect on their own behaviour and learning (Revans, 1971). This approach, now known as Action Learning, has influenced many subsequent management development programmes in Britain as well as Belgium. The emphasis on action, combined with exchange of ideas and theory as problems were encountered, is not dissimilar to the 'guided discovery learning' ideas of the Industrial Training Research Unit. The real skill for the tutor/trainer is to ensure that theory and practice come together at a time and in a way that the learner can handle and put to good use.

Individual preference in learning method

Other researchers and activists in the area of management development were working to throw more light on learning and development. One of the professors in the USA who had some contact with the participants in Revans' Belgian group was David Kolb, whose work on the stages in a potential cycle of learning and problem solving is now well known (Kolb, 1984). In Britain there have been initiatives to provide a means of measuring preferred learning styles and to enable each individual to take action to find more effective ways of learning and managing (Honey and Mumford, 1992).

Much of this work leads to the same conclusion of a classification of four stages or styles that can be involved in learning:

A *Action/Experience:*   those with limited success in academic studies will often feel more comfortable with this starting point, though some well-educated managers with a leaning towards operations and customer contact are also drawn to methods which involve them in action.

B *Reflection/Reviewing:*   some people feel the need to discuss experiences and observe the actions of others. Action without reflection can often lead to repeated mistakes and limited learning for other situations. Too much reflection can inhibit movement towards new action.

C *Theory/Conceptualizing:*   many academic courses and students assume that this is the main aim of their efforts—trying to find the means of summarizing the phenomena in the world or in human thought. Those working in business usually have some concepts which guide their endeavours, though industries, organizations and individuals vary in the importance they give to this area, particularly in Britain.

D *Experimenting/Trying it out:*   in business life, theory is only useful if it enables people to find some new product or way of operating. On the other hand, those who stay in this experimenting mode and do not move into the action and then reflect on it may launch a succession of expensive initiatives and mistakes.

Although some people have used this kind of classification to identify their (or others') preferred way of learning and have even tried to develop some learning styles which are comparatively weak, Kolb clearly advocates a cyclical approach where one seeks to move around the stages in sequence A–B–C–D–A, etc. This certainly enables the link between theory and practice to be made in a reliable way, ensuring that understanding is deepened with every completion of the cycle. We have designed learning events that use this cyclical approach, and for most people this seems to meet their needs and is welcomed in a post-experience group; the only exception was someone from a highly technological firm who wanted to have all the theory and nothing but theory—the opportunity to see it in action and reflect on such experience did not suit this person.

A definition of development

At last we may have arrived at a definition of development. From what we have been saying we can now offer the following:

> **Development occurs when a gain in experience is effectively combined with the conceptual understanding that can illuminate it, giving increased confidence both to act and to perceive how such action relates to its context.**

This definition clearly differentiates development from training which need not have a link with experience and may not give attention to contexts, though in some cases it may do. Learning that has not been tried out in experience is unlikely to give increased confidence in action—the cycle is incomplete. Similarly, experience that has not been reflected on and fitted into its conceptual context will give limited confidence to act in different situations.

Development that fulfils the above definition is often seen to have a maturing effect on people, as is often seen in participants in the part-time self-managed learning MBA at Roffey Park (Cunningham, 1991) where participants take responsibility, under monitored conditions, for applying their learning in action in their work situations and have to reflect and report on the results of this to a group of peers in a learning 'set'. Thus development is likely to involve more than cognitive learning: it has a personal involvement through experiencing some challenge or emotional risk and being willing to reflect on it or be observed and receive feedback. Because of the involvement in experience it will be likely to link in with the environment and the changes going on in the person's organization.

Assessment and development

We are now in a position to fit together the concepts and activities of assessment and development. Earlier in this chapter we made brief reference to an assessment and development project for one of the biggest Portuguese banks, and this was an excellent example of how one activity needed the other: assessment without development would have left the individuals stranded without achieving the intended transition, and development without assessment would have lacked a basis and a clarification of need.

Any assessment (or self-assessment) gives possibilities for change and development. Only a small minority of people are assessed as *exactly* matching the roles and careers being considered (as will be shown in the information from Belgium in Chapter 5), so immediately there is scope for development. In addition, with the changes happening in the business world there will be possibilities for everyone to define some experience or skill which they need to acquire.

In this book we try to take a broad look at assessment and development, but even in this chapter it may be obvious that the assessment centre method has a tendency to predominate in our interests. This is because it has become clear in recent years that the framework and potential encompassed by the assessment centre approach allow the use of whatever exercise, test or enquiry may best enable assessment and then development to occur.

Assessment/development centres are the *starting point* for development, and in most cases the benefit from the activity only begins when the feedback of data is done. With some development centres, feedback is given after each exercise, particularly in peer assessment, but usually there is a need to integrate the data and *translate* the result into a form helpful for feedback, i.e.:

Translate
Assessment data - - - - - - - - - - - - - - - -> Stimulus for development

For example, 'A low level of participation and effectiveness in the group discussion' needs to be expressed in terms of possible development of skills of assertiveness, though the form of that development would need to be discussed with the person before any definitive plans were made.

There are those who try to define the boundary between assessment centres and development centres (Lee and Beard, 1994), but this seems an unnecessary division and one that is not supported by practice where the terms used are chosen more to suit company politics than to fit any set of rules defined by someone else.

Although various development programmes have been designed without systematic prior assessment of individual or group needs, there is now seen to be an increasingly important link between such assessment and a successful development plan or programme. Not only should there be a link at the level of content, but also at the motivational level, so that whoever is undertaking a form of development has been able to see that there is new experience/skill/knowledge to be gained and to make a commitment to this development. This is where the feedback and self-assessment which are available through a properly designed assessment or development centre can give a firm starting point for planning and action.

A well-known guide to self-development for managers (Pedler, Burgoyne and Boydell, 3e, 1994) devotes much of Part 1 of the book to setting goals and assessing oneself, and this is much to be commended. Many people, however, find it difficult to do this on their own, and the opportunity to take part in a challenging, but supportive, event like an assessment centre where trained observers focus their attention on the abilities of the few participants is a priceless gift which can be turned into valuable and lasting development for the individuals and for the organization that provides it. We make no apologies for our commitment to this work of adding value!

Key points, limitations and principles for success

1 Each country has particular strengths in assessment and development, some of which are based on thoroughly developed expertise, but there is also need for validation studies and questions in relation to assumptions made with some methods.
2 Managers in organizations tend to favour methods of which they already have experience. This may limit the speed at which newer, better validated methods can be introduced. Human resource specialists should take every opportunity to provide information on improved methods.
3 Assessment centre methodology is increasingly seen as improving validity in assessment and as providing a helpful starting point for development in which the participants are provided with full information and clarity about their role in planning the development.
4 Development needs to relate theory with practice in an integrated way, based closely on the changing business environment and the abilities that are needed in order to flourish amidst these challenges. Methods that use the motivation of individuals are likely to work best.
5 Being able to draw on a variety of methods of assessment and development to suit the circumstances, the culture and the country is essential. This makes increasingly heavy demands on human resources staff within companies who will need to draw on external expertise to supplement their own and to convince senior management that new methods may have relevance.

References and further reading

Almeida, L.S. and Ribeiro, S.I. (1991) 'Porquê falar em avaliação e em testes psicológicos', paper presented at the annual conference of the Association of Portuguese Psychologists.

Anstey, E. (1977) 'A 30-year follow-up of the CSSB procedure, with lessons for the future', *Journal of Occupational Psychology*, 50, 149–159.

Anstey, E. (1989) 'Reminiscences of a Wartime Army Psychologist', *The Psychologist*, November 1989, 475–478.

Belbin, R.M. (1969) *The Discovery Method in Training*, Training Information Paper 5, HMSO, London (republished 1979 by Training Services Division, MSC).

Cunningham, I. (1991) 'Self-managed learning' in Mumford, A. (ed.) *Handbook of Management Development*, third edition, Gower, Aldershot.

Department of Employment (1972) *Training for the future: a plan for discussion*, HMSO, London.

Downs, S. (1985) *Testing Trainability*, NFER-NELSON, Windsor.

Ernoult, V., Gruère, J-P. and Pezeu, F. (1984) *Le Bilan Comportemental dans l'entreprise*, Presses Universitaires de France, Paris.

Honey, P. and Mumford, A. (1992) *The Manual of Learning Styles*, third edition, Honey, London.

Jeserich, W. (1981) *Mitarbeiter auswählen und fördern*—Assessment Center Verfahren, Carl Hanser Verlag, München.

Kolb, D. (1984) *Experiential Learning: experience as the source of learning and development*, Prentice-Hall, Englewood Cliffs, N.J.

Lee, G. and Beard, D. (1994) *Development Centres: realizing the potential of your employees through assessment and development*, McGraw-Hill, Maidenhead.

Pedler, M., Burgoyne, J. and Boydell, T. (3e, 1994) *A Manager's Guide to Self-development*, McGraw-Hill, Maidenhead.

Pillat, R. (1986) *Neue Mitarbeiter erfolgreich anwerben, auswählen und einsetzen*, S.206–214, Rudolf Haufe Verlag, Freiburg im Breisgau.

Rawling, K. (1985) *The Seven Point Plan: new perspectives 50 years on*, NFER-NELSON, Windsor.

Revans, R.W. (1971) *Developing Effective Managers: a new approach to business education*, Praeger, New York.

Ribeiro, R. (1993) 'Selection Methods: Theoretical Solutions versus Portuguese Reality', paper presented at the first meeting on Organizational Behaviour, Instituto Superior de Psicologia Aplicada, Lisbon.

Shackleton, V. and Newell, S. (1993) 'How companies in Europe select their managers', *Selection and Development Review*, Vol. 9, No. 6.

Stewart, A. and Stewart, V. (1981) *Tomorrow's Managers Today*, Institute of Personnel Management, London.

Thornton, G.C. and Byham, W.C. (1982) *Assessment Centers and Managerial Performance*, Academic Press, New York.

2 Assessment centres in action

Ulrike Hess, Mac Bolton and Jan Gijswijt

In this chapter we will present some features of three projects which will build up a picture of assessment centres as used in different parts of Europe for purposes of assessment, placement, development and restructuring of staff in various kinds of organizations.

Through these cases a number of principles will be illustrated and at the end of the chapter these will be brought together and summarized so that the learning from the experiences can be made explicit.

The current demands of human resource management are to be seen at various points, and the need for careful attention to training and development is as vital as the requirement for expertise in assessment methods: assessment centres depend on well-trained observers, role-players and assessors for their reliability, and the follow-up needs sophistication in applying developmental methods.

Some of the key factors to watch out for in each of these projects are:

- Why was the assessment centre method used?
- What were the special benefits achieved by the method?
- What expertise was needed to deliver the benefits?
- What training did it depend on?
- What development did the participants gain?
- What development did the observers/assessors gain?

We report on the setting up of a new factory in Germany, a promotion/development project in Britain, and assessment and development to assist the privatization of an organization in Holland. The cases cover manufacturing, distribution and a service organization, with a number of challenging features in each.

Selection for a lean production company

This section of the chapter is a report on the selection procedure for employees—especially skilled workers—of a company for its newly erected production plant according to the company's philosophy of lean production.

The company under consideration manufactures motor cars. It decided to build a production plant which was to be one of the most modern and progressive car factories in Europe.

The lean production philosophy stands for manufacturing competitive products of high quality at low cost and at the same time creating employment that is economically secure and caters for human needs. To achieve this, certain prerequisites must be met for the type of production and for the specific abilities of all employees.

We will deal only briefly with the technological and technical prerequisites, although they are most certainly connected with the abilities of employees who are working with this technology.

The report concentrates mainly on the description of the company's expectations and requirements of its future employees and on methods applied for the selection of suitable people.

A principle of lean production is outsourcing, i.e. to hire other companies for services, even on a large scale, and to create a close relationship with them. As an example of applying this principle the company assigned the task of selecting all employees on its behalf to a consulting institute (Team für Psychologisches Management). This also included the administration of all personnel data by means of a personnel information computer program, which was specially designed for this task.

Values   One possible way of defining what is required of employees is to look at the 'values' of the company. These are the company's guidelines for the definition of goals and their application.

The following values are named for this company:

- *customer orientation*   There are external customers (suppliers, municipalities, clients, etc.) and internal customers (employees, teams, departments, etc.). Customers will be content if their expectations are satisfied with regard to quality, security, technology, etc.
- *teamwork*   The 'we' is the centre of working with each other. Mutual support, taking over responsibilities, replacing each other as well as establishing and maintaining contact with others are the basic principles of teamwork.
- *continuous improvement*   Continuous improvement in production and administration by creative ideas and by analyses of reflections on profitability, effectiveness and productivity is called for. Suggestions for improvement are put into effect with determination. Employees are encouraged to be wide awake and active.
- *open communication*

    —Open communication and mutual trust must be established with all partners. Open communication provides an extensive flow of information and thus the prerequisite for customer orientation, continuous improvement and the formation of teamwork.

—Open-plan offices and the use of written media within and outside the company are fundamental elements.

—The communication should be bi-directional both on a personal level and between all hierarchy levels during the various regular meetings (daily meetings of teams, departments, areas).

—The works council will be involved in all management activities.

● *development of the employee's personal responsibility*

—Prior to employment all employees will take part in intensive technical and company-specific training.

—All employees will be continuously trained in seminars on subjects such as problem solving, communication, etc. They learn to take over personal responsibility increasingly in their work and are constantly reminded of this philosophy.

—Job rotation, enlargement and enrichment strategies help to make the work more attractive. To enjoy work is an important value.

Principles of work organization

Certain principles for the work organization can be deduced from the company's values:

1 *Continuous improvement*   Continuous improvement affects the work organization not only during daily team meetings which always have 'improvement' on the agenda; but it also becomes the responsibility of the team leader to stimulate others to think in terms of improvement suggestions and to ensure that the necessary action is taken. Continuous improvement puts the main emphasis on preventive acting, which helps to recognize mistakes in time and to rectify them. It begins with tracking and elimination of waste (e.g. by overproduction, stock in storage, transfer of material and employees, waiting periods, mistakes).

2 *Quality*   Another characteristic of the work organization is the awareness of quality. The definition of quality is that the features of a product must comply with set standards. Every employee is responsible for checking the quality of his or her work. Apart from technical control and fault indicating systems, the attitude of each employee towards his or her work is decisive, i.e. to achieve high standards (principle of zero mistakes), preventive intervention and personal checks. A quality control department becomes almost redundant, since all employees are called upon to ensure the high quality of their work.

3 *Task of managers*   The task of a manager is not only to ensure stability and continuity within the department, but also to be flexible to changing requirements and to initiate and drive forward changes. Successful management is described as follows:

—Open-mindedness and trust are results of the extensive exchange of information and communication between managers and groups. Further tasks are the setting of clear goals, planning the means and controlling, as well as reflecting on, the steps that lead to these

goals. Managers also have to live up to the image of being open
to criticism and of accepting others.

—Teamwork and management are brought into line, so that the
groups together with their manager take responsibility for the
work and decision process. The manager assigns jobs to the group
and the group then plans the work itself.

Since job enrichment, enlargement and rotation as well as hierarchical
promotion are basic values of the company, the manager should
recognize and use the possibilities for personal development of each
employee.

4 *Teamwork*   The whole company is run by various teams, e.g. in
assembly, production control or management. Teamwork
characterizes the culture of the company to a large extent.
The teams in the production line consist of between four and ten
members. A team leader is elected for each group according to a
specified procedure. The team leader acts as presenter, spokesperson
and coordinator and is responsible for certain tasks. The chief
engineer delegates the work to the *whole* team and is authorized to
issue directives to the team. He or she agrees on goals, sees to it that
they are carried out and acts as disciplinary supervisor. The
responsibility for completing a task is shared by the team leader and
the team. In other words, the teams take responsibility for their own
work as semi-autonomous groups. The various teams have a
supplier–customer relationship with each other. This means that only
top quality goods or services are supplied to another group. It is also
essential for the individual to understand other people's tasks. In
addition, the teams should be able to support each other. This means
that everyone must be prepared for and capable of understanding
and performing other tasks (i.e. replacing each other).

5 *Flat hierarchy*   The flat hierarchy is closely connected with the
groupwork. In total there are five levels; anyone can approach
anyone else, whether they are from the same level or not. In
bottleneck situations even managers help out at the production line.
An exterior sign of the approachability to colleagues and employees
from other departments and levels is the work uniform that
everybody wears. No suits or ties are worn in management.

The way in which the values of the company and the principles of work
organization fit together is illustrated and summarized in Table 2.1.

With this knowledge of the lean production philosophy, the consulting
institute on the one hand had to develop criteria for a selection procedure according to which the suitability of applicants for a position as
skilled worker could be assessed. On the other hand, exercises and tasks
had to be found that would reflect typical situations of the future job.

Furthermore, it was essential to take a close look at the group of
prospective applicants to see whether their qualifications and work

Table 2.1 *The lean production values and principles of work organization*

Values	Principles of work organization
• Customer orientation	Quality
• Personal responsibility	
• Continuous improvement	Daily continuous improvement meetings
• Teamwork	The whole company is run by various teams
• Open communication	Specified tasks of managers
	Flat hierarchy

experience would comply with the requirements. Further thought went into the acceptability of the procedure to the participants.

Criteria for the selection procedure

The following criteria for the procedure were finally developed:

- *Manual dexterity and technical understanding/recognition of logical coherence*   Since the plant has a highly complex technology, the employees are expected to show manual dexterity. For example, they have to work at conveyor belts or with computer-controlled robots in the paint and bodywork areas. Technological understanding is necessary for the maintenance of machines and plant equipment, since each employee is responsible for his or her quality-orientated work. To carry out the work correctly, especially when computer-based technology is involved, technical understanding and recognizing logical coherence are essential for the employees.
- *Cooperation and communication*   Good social skills are necessary not only for teamwork, but also for contact with other employees, for team leader functions and for realizing the concept of customer orientation.
- *Initiative/flexibility*   Deduced from the concept of continuous improvement, applicants are expected to reflect on their work independently, not to be content with the standard achieved, and to strive for better results. Apart from showing initiative, flexible thinking and acting are essential for adaptation to ever-changing working conditions.
- *Perseverance and the ability to cope with stress*   In addition to the above requirements it is important to evaluate perseverance and the ability to cope with stress, since the work is demanding on both body and mind. These abilities are important criteria during assessment, since they may not necessarily have been called for to this extent in other jobs.

- *Professional motivation*   Professional motivation is another criterion for selection, i.e. what motivates applicants to apply for the job, what expectancies do they have, what efforts are they prepared to make, to what extent have they informed themselves about the company, etc.

Design of suitable exercises   The second part of development of a selection procedure entailed the design of suitable exercises and tasks which on the one hand would reflect working situations as realistically as possible and on the other hand would be experienced by applicants as challenging and would be taken seriously.

The selection procedure is divided into two stages: the pre-selection, and the assessment centre.

The aim of the *pre-selection* is to give applicants information on the process of recruitment, the system of production and the work organization. During this selection stage, information on the motivation of the applicant and on his or her technical and methodical know-how is gathered.

The following exercises are implemented:

- *Group discussion*   In this exercise five participants form a group. They are given a task, e.g. to build a model car according to certain criteria (price, design, stability) with parts from a construction kit. Once they have finished the product, a reflection phase follows and together they look at mistakes made and discuss possible improvements. During this exercise the participants are assessed on their ability to communicate and cooperate and also on how well they succeed in transforming the instructions given into working methods. Motivation in these situations is also determined.
- *Introduction exercise*   In this exercise the participants have to describe their career, interests and qualifications. The observers can supplement this information by asking questions. The aim of the exercise is to determine the technical aptitude of the participants and to obtain detailed information, e.g. on specialized know-how and technical training.
- *Psychological tests*   The third part of the pre-selection includes psychological tests, all of which are paper and pencil tests. These measure the logical thinking, mechanical/technical understanding, three-dimensional powers of imagination and the concentration ability of the applicant.

Each participant is given personal feedback on the assessment of each exercise, together with the results.

Successful applicants are invited to an assessment centre which takes place one or two weeks later.

The aim of the *assessment centre* is to gather information on the applicant's social competence and his or her manual skills and dexterity. It includes the following exercises:

- *Group exercise*   After an initial introduction the assessment centre, like the pre-selection, begins with an exercise which the group carries out together. However, unlike the group exercise in the pre-selection, it asks for more decisions to be taken by the group. Apart from the ability to cooperate, participants are assessed here on the degree of responsibility and commitment shown during their performance, and on their quality-orientated work.

- *Construction exercise*   During this exercise the participants are divided into three groups. The task for all three groups is to build a specific object together. Each group builds one part of the object. To ensure that the different parts fit together, various phases are scheduled during which the groups coordinate with each other (by means of representatives).

    The aim of the exercise is to assess the communication skills between the teams, i.e. how well a participant is able to inform others about the results of his or her group, in turn receiving new information for implementation by his or her group. Furthermore, the exercise shows the participant's ability to work independently, to adhere exactly to a given time schedule and his or her ability to think cross-functionally.

- *Assembly exercise*   This part of the assessment centre consists of two practical exercises. During the first exercise participants have to assemble a mechanical object consisting of various parts by following written instructions. The instructions specify that the object has to be handed over to a waiting customer. As in other exercises a time limit is set.

    This exercise shows how quickly and precisely the participant works manually. It also shows whether a participant is able to grasp the written instructions and put them into action. The completed object is tested for its quality (reliability according to various tests) and the quantity (time taken for the assembly) is also recorded. Applicants are also assessed on the tidiness and cleanliness of their work.

    All these criteria can be fully related to the future employment. Therefore this exercise has high validity and high predictive value. The second exercise also evaluates manual skills. Here the emphasis is on routine tasks. Two metal blades have to be put together with a set amount of screws, nuts and washers. As many blades as possible must be assembled within a set time.

    Both speed and precision of the work as well as optimizing the assembly procedure and manual skills are observed. The participant's endurance and ability to cope with stress can be assessed, and cleanliness and tidiness at work are also evaluated.

- *Reflection*   This exercise follows the assembly. During individual interviews participants are asked by observers to reflect on their work during the assembly exercise and to assess themselves. They are given the opportunity to say what they would improve the next time or what could be improved in general.

Table 2.2   *The criteria and exercises of assessment centres*

Criteria	Exercises
• Manual dexterity and technical understanding • Cooperation and communication • Initiative • Perseverance • Professional motivation	• Paper-and-pencil tests for intellectual and technical understanding • Assembly exercises • Group exercises • Teams working together • Reflection exercise • Personal interview

The continuous improvement principle forms part of this exercise. Participants are assessed on their ability to evaluate their own work and also on their ability to develop suggestions for their improvement.

The criteria used in selection and the associated exercises are summarized in Table 2.2.

Feedback and results

As before, the assessment centre is followed up by feedback to each participant. The observers report to them on their behaviour as observed and assessed during each exercise. Applicants are then informed whether or not a job is offered to them.

After these two stages of the selection procedure the applicants have to undergo a company medical examination. In addition, the chief engineers get the opportunity to interview those applicants who will be employed in their department in the future and to obtain more details on the applicants' qualifications.

Within two years 2000 employees were selected from 10 000 applicants by this procedure. The success of the company proves that the 'right' employees were selected. In future this selection procedure will also be implemented to fill vacancies arising due to natural fluctuations.

Assessment for development for distribution management

One of the major uses of the assessment centre method has always been to identify people already within an organization for a more demanding role which they have not yet filled. One of the early uses of the method was for identifying from the ranks of the armed services those who had the potential for being trained as officers (Anstey, 1989). There has been a strong growth of interest in this method in British business organizations during the past 15 years and the example given here is representative of several applications of the development of the method from pioneer work in Britain and in the USA.

In this case, based in distribution of dairy products to retail outlets, the company saw the need to be able to expand the number of distribution centres to meet growing demand for their products from retailers throughout Britain. Some of these centres were the existing regional depots, but others would be new centres serving particular national retail organizations. An increase in the number of distribution managers would be needed to meet the expected expansion and it was not clear whether candidates could be identified by conventional appraisal and promotion methods. Although the company had the support of its parent group of companies, the role of distribution manager in this part of the group needed experience and interest in its specialist distribution activities to commercial retail organizations. Warehouse managers and transport managers could be potential candidates for development to meet the need, but the problem was how to identify those who had the potential to do the job.

The seven regional managers were the people most concerned with providing effectively for future needs and they were keen to identify suitable candidates from within the company before following the alternative path of recruiting experienced distribution managers from outside. One of the regional managers had had previous contact with Roffey Park and had heard of the assessment centre method. The regional managers authorized two of their number to work with Roffey Park in designing an assessment centre to meet the objective of developing a stock of future distribution managers. Two personnel and training staff were also involved in setting up and running the assessment centre, but this case is probably unusual in that the main impetus to use the method came from the regional managers, who showed strong support for the work needed to set it in motion.

Development of criteria

The first task, as always, was to obtain agreement on the process of establishing the criteria for competent performance of a distribution manager. As the role already existed at the regional distribution centres, the relevant data could be obtained by diagnostic interviews with the regional managers to whom the existing (and new) roles reported. It would be important to take account of any impending changes in the roles and any wider business trends: these were discussed with two people at head office who were best placed to predict these. The method developed at Roffey Park for defining managerial jobs and careers was used (Bolton, 1986), which draws on personal construct theory and what is usually known as 'repertory grid' methods, though the classic work of George Kelly was in a different field (Kelly, 1955, republished 1991). The method as used in this case involved the following:

1 Arranging interviews with each of the regional managers, their manager and a head office planning manager.
2 The investigator visited most of these people in their offices on various sites, having asked for two hours to be set aside without interruptions for each interview.
3 The pattern of interviewing included asking each person interviewed to identify some above-average performers and some not-so-good

performers in the role. An above-average performer was then contrasted with a not-so-good performer and the interviewee asked to describe three areas of behaviour that were important and on which the former person performed better than the latter.

4 Further information was obtained by following the same personal construct principles applied to how the above-average performer spends more time on three activities than the not-so-good performer. Again, the same method was used in comparing how these pairs of people dealt with critical incidents.

5 The 106 constructs from these interviews were clustered using a 'cluster map' approach to enable integrated definitions of 21 identifiable criteria to be obtained, defined in behavioural terms. These definitions were then listed in random order, without headings, and were sent to those who had been interviewed who were then asked to rank them in order of importance and return them with any comments they had (see the box below which shows the covering letter used).

6 From the average rank order derived from the regional managers' lists and from their comments, a refined list of 12 agreed criteria was obtained, which was accepted by the company as defining effective performance for distribution managers. The average rank order also gave a basis for weighting some criteria as more important than others.

Request to rank order the 'constructs'

Each person interviewed has contributed to the attached combined list of abilities which featured in considering the job performance of distribution managers and similar managers.

In order to help us to refine this list so that we can end up with about 10 criteria for measurement in the assessment centre, please put them in order from 1 to 21 ('1' being the most important, in your opinion, and '21' being the least important). I know that this is a difficult task. To make it a little easier I suggest you first divide the 21 into three groups of about seven in each, so that:

> A = Extremely important
> B = Very important
> C = Important or not so important

Then within each of the three groups you should be able to identify a rank order. Please try to avoid making two or more of equal rank—try to come to a decision, even if it is rather arbitrary.

It would be most helpful if you could end up with a rank

---

order such that the numbers 1 to 21 are spread over the 21 constructs, marked in the left-hand margin.

Then, if you have any comments to make on the content of the constructs please note them on the third sheet.

Many thanks.

Mac Bolton

Design of programme and exercises

Having obtained a manageable list of criteria which are based on the reality of present and future needs, it is then possible to begin to design the assessment centre. No assumptions are made beforehand about the nature of the exercises which need to be based firmly on finding the best way of measuring people against the detailed criteria. It is usually convenient to use headings for the criteria, but these are merely codes indicating the substance within each definition. In using the criteria as an observer one must always keep looking closely at the precise descriptions of the behaviour being sought.

A matrix of exercises against criteria is constructed which aims to ensure that:

- each main criterion has at least one exercise that has been specifically designed to elicit the defined behaviour in it
- each criterion is observed in at least two or three different exercises, ideally mirroring the contexts encountered in the job, e.g. written work, one-to-one or group
- each exercise will usually enable more than one criterion to be assessed, often up to five or six, otherwise the assessment centre will be too long and complex.

In this case, assessment information was collected in eight different ways, although mostly in only three ways for each criterion. The matrix shown in Figure 2.1 gives an outline of how this was done.

The progressive case study

As seen in Figure 2.1 there was a major case study exercise running through the assessment centre where in each phase a different person was put in a leadership position with a team of three other people whom they would lead and control. This exercise was needed to elicit the behaviour defined in Criterion 2, 'Delegates but controls'. An In-tray exercise and Questionnaire could give an indication of how people *think about* delegating and express it on paper, but only a practical exercise that involves instructing and controlling others would be reliably predictive of how they would behave in the real job. The situation used as the case material was designed to simulate the demands of the distribution manager role in delegating and controlling, although it was an analogous context—that of running a youth water

Criteria	Progressive case study *L	*T	In-tray & interview	Problems I	II	Interview	Questionnaire	Assessment by current manager
1. More profit from work			✓	✓	✓	✓		
2. Delegates but controls	✓		✓				✓	
3. Degrees of priority	✓		✓					✓
4. Plans for future			✓	✓		✓		
5. Options for decision	✓		✓	✓	✓			
6. Determination					✓	✓		✓
7. Satisfies the client		✓	✓	✓				
8. Faces industrial relations issues			✓	✓				
9. Motivates staff	✓					✓		✓
10. Helps people perform	✓		✓			✓		✓
11. Realizes they are a team		✓			✓			
12. Lucid confidence	✓				✓	✓		

*L = observation of the person leading the team in a particular phase of the case study
*T = observation of the team members

Figure 2.1 *Matrix of exercises against criteria*

sports centre. Each phase was different and, although the basic context was the same, there was a new brief each time which was not dependent on the results of the previous phase. Also as the case progressed, interspersed with other kinds of exercises, the briefs increased in complexity in order to balance the learning from previous phases. This was an attempt to be fair in the challenge given to each of the four people in each group. (The assessment centre was actually run with two groups of four people, alternating their involvement with the progressive case study.)

The person in the lead was observed on the behaviour defined by six of the criteria which the exercise and brief were specifically designed to test. The three other team members were observed on two other criteria as shown in the matrix. Each of the criteria was always observed using the full definition: as an example the 'Delegates but controls' definition was:

Delegates by identifying clearly what needs to be done, briefing immediate subordinates very clearly on targets, laying the ground rules, systems and plans for them to operate and allowing them to work out solutions rather than managing it for them, but retains control by taking steps to review objectives and evaluate results.

Other exercises The remainder of the exercises shown in the matrix are more conventional. Problems I was a set of written problems, each testing one of the five criteria designated in the matrix. The second part of the exercise, Problems II, was a leaderless group discussion where the four people in the group shared responsibility for reaching consensus on the best solution to four of the problems, each person taking a turn at presenting the initial proposal for dealing with one problem.

The assessment report asked for from each participant's current manager may seem surprising, and contrary to the view often held that information from outside the assessment centre should be excluded. In this application, however, the participants were all already at managerial level within the company, performing jobs which in some respects demanded the abilities being assessed, such as in dealing with industrial relations problems. The purpose of the assessment centre was largely developmental so it was important to draw in all information which would show not only the potential for future performance but also what had, or had not, been shown in these respects in their current roles. Special reports were called for from the regional managers (or in one or two cases other senior managers at head office or in other divisions if participants were employed elsewhere than in the regional organizations). Information was thus requested on five criteria where current performance was likely to be predictive of future ability. These reports were not made available to observers until the appropriate point of the evaluation meeting after the assessment centre, and were always compared carefully against other observations to ensure that there was no undue bias. This procedure seemed to work well and improved the data available for assessing development needs.

Training for observing, assessing and developing The company was quick to recognize the importance of training, and the four chosen observers/assessors (two regional managers and two personnel and training staff) were asked to set aside three days for training before the first assessment centre was held. The date had to be postponed once to ensure that all four could attend together. Similarly, there were delays to the holding of the first assessment centre. This indicates one of the limitations of the assessment centre method in that it is usually necessary for quite a large number of people to be brought together at one place and time. As we became clearer on the potential benefits to be obtained from the whole project, the decision was taken to have two training modules, one of three days and the other of two days. The purpose of this was to meet the need:

- to equip the assessor team in observing, assessing and evaluating the data
- to go into considerable depth on the feedback process and on how to stimulate development for improved performance and career progression.

The two modules were divided according to these respective needs and the second module took place *after* the first assessment centre was held so that specific attention could be given to feedback and development using the examples of the participants who thus formed live case studies.

In providing the first module an important principle was that the observers/assessors should experience the whole process of observing and assessing as part of the training so that they would be able to appreciate the need for reliable reporting of their observations to the other team members. Once this whole process has been experienced, observers are better able to perceive the need for full, accurate recording of the relevant behaviour. There is nothing like being challenged in the evaluation meeting for making one aware of the need for recording data at the time of the event. Training needs to provide some knowledge about the assessment centre process, but it must also develop the skill of the observers so that when they first observe genuine participants they have progressed a long way up the 'learning curve' in order to guarantee reliable observations. The first module for the company covered the following areas:

- the process of designing an assessment centre
- the criteria: source, meaning and relative weighting
- how exercises measure the criteria: the matrix
- skills of observation: practice with video-tape
- the division of tasks between observers
- the in-tray exercise and in-tray interviewing skills
- semi-structured interviewing and practice
- mini-assessment centre with 'actor' participants
- marking and preparation for evaluation
- evaluation meeting: focus on the process
- briefing for the full assessment centre programme.

The advantage of using 'actor' participants, i.e. people who are not expecting any subsequent involvement or feedback for development purposes, is that the observers can make mistakes and learn from the process without anyone's career being affected. The actors are asked to give honest feedback after the experience so that the organizers can make improvements to the programme before the first real event. Another advantage of this 'trial' event is that it is not necessary to complete the evaluation of all the data—the time in the evaluation meeting (sometimes called the 'wash-up') is used to enable the observers/assessors to learn in depth about the process rather than having to focus on the results.

The second training module used in this case had a very practical format as it was able to use the actual results from the first assessment centre, but there was also a need to share perceptions of development policy, company needs and how to integrate individual aspirations with the reality of what was possible. The programme of this second module was:

- career development: organizational need, individual aspirations and the reality of career paths
- integrating the data from different sources; certainty, doubt and knowing the level of reliability
- the cases, preparation for practical work
- two cases, role-played and reviewed with video-tape
- training and development plans: roles of line managers, personnel staff, mentors and career counsellors
- learning styles and how they may vary
- three more cases, role-played and reviewed.

After the second training module the four assessors each went to the locations of two of the participants in the first assessment centre and carried out a feedback/development interview to assist the participants in putting together development and career plans using the information that was now available to them. Having the opportunity to role-play the cases was a unique benefit not available to subsequent cases and enabled the team to gain detailed knowledge of how each assessor would be likely to approach each interview. Advice was shared in an open way.

The reality of the assessment centre and its evaluation

Measuring the success of this kind of event is never easy, and especially when the purpose is largely developmental where many other influences are at work. The project was intended to provide an answer to a temporary need for increased numbers of distribution managers, preferably by internal development or transfer within the company. All potential candidates for development participated in the events, which ran smoothly and were perceived as challenging but relevant to the purpose. All had follow-up discussions with carefully chosen assessors from the team, matching the assessors to the individuals as far as possible and ensuring that line managers were kept informed. It is difficult to measure the value to the individuals of such discussions, but there is no doubt that the quality of such information is much higher than any development discussions held without it. Individuals, and the company, are better able to take decisions about training and development initiatives or do so with greater chance of success. Following the assessment centre a few individuals were promoted fairly quickly, some embarked on a process of development and a few decided that they were not likely to succeed in development within the company and opted for a career move externally in due course. It could be argued that these decisions might not have been very different if the assessment centre had not been held, but the real benefit is in the increase in confidence in such decisions, not only for the company but also for the individuals; and the hidden benefit is that individuals, as a result of the feedback, are able to feel much more involved in their own development and more in control of their employability, both within the company and outside.

An extra benefit is the learning that the observers/assessors gain from the preparatory training and from taking part in a team of people setting high standards in the assessment and development of others. One of the regional managers who took part in this way subsequently made a career move into a human resource development role within the company.

Assessment and development in privatization

This case is a description of the experience of a Dutch administrative company which we will call Mercure, using assessment centre methods to help achieve the transition towards new policies and activities. At the time there were almost 6000 men and 2500 women working full-time for the company. In addition, there were almost 2500 men and women working part-time.

The company had merged five years previously, incorporating three state institutions and becoming privatized at the same time. At that time provision was made for new activities to be added to the traditional ones, and further developments for the future were outlined and agreed upon as possible areas with growth potential. It was not only the content of the activities which was changing, but even more important the policy and philosophy of the new emerging organization were in transition; Mercure had to change because it had left the protection of being a unique state institute and had moved towards the competitive open environment where it had to make its own living and even ensure its survival in a hostile environment. This required a total change of approach from a government service orientation towards the results orientation of a competitive profit-making organization.

Another important change happening at this time, though seemingly a side issue, was that the privatized company had to cope with a past where much of the work (of a coding nature) had been done by less educated people. This coding work was now disappearing and it was difficult to find alternative jobs for these people. Continuing automation would be likely to exacerbate these problems in the near future.

Summarizing the situation, we see that the merger and the privatization were made more complicated because of:

- changing/new activities
- fast-developing technology
- changing from a product focus towards a market orientation
- a forced pace of commercialization
- changing from a service attitude towards an output orientation.

Assessment centres for promotion

The many changes being faced raised the question of whether or not new management and staff should be attracted from outside, or whether they could also be found from within the organization. One of the ways in which the organization tried to meet the need was the selection of promising young people from the company's rank and file. All those who were interested could participate in the selection procedure and, in addition, managers and supervisors were able to encourage those who in their eyes might qualify to apply for this special programme.

After a first rough selection about 60 candidates were selected to pass through a more refined process. The remaining 24 candidates then had to undergo a two-day assessment centre, after which 50 per cent were finally admitted into the one-year development programme. All the participants received feedback and useful additional information about the way in which their performance during the simulations was assessed. They were given the opportunity to compare and confront these findings with their own feelings and reactions, and they were also given the chance to decide on priorities for improvement and to find ways and means of implementing such improvement.

Those selected for the one-year development programme had a series of three- or five-day training periods alternated with their normal work in their own departments, and they were also placed in other departments for some periods. The series of modules, fitted in according to candidates' needs, began shortly after the assessment centre took place, and candidates were then expected to reformulate their now matured ideas about their personal learning needs.

Was the programme considered successful?

The participants were expected to complete evaluation sheets on a regular basis and what they said was generally positive, but it must be recognized that that could just reflect the happy feeling of having been 'selected' and predestined for a promising job. And was it purely a question of the quality of the procedure or was it partly a self-fulfilling prophecy that the participants had already been chosen and recruited before the end of the programme by departments that were in need of promising leadership? Those who organized the procedure probably learned more from what was not in the evaluation sheets than from the recorded views, as illustrated below.

Not perfect

Strikingly enough, all the candidates experienced the assessment centre as an interesting experience, the 'accepted' ones being somewhat more positive than the 'rejected' ones, as measured shortly after the selection procedure. It was only by accident, however, that someone from the training staff overheard many months later a conversation that indicated that some very friendly contacts between candidates, which had been made before the assessment centre took place, had been broken off since that event. It seemed that several of the unsuccessful candidates had experienced this selection procedure as a failure to such an extent that they did not want to stay in touch with colleagues who had been accepted. This seemed very harmful, not only for the candidates but also for the organization where barriers had appeared between employees who might meet again at any time or might even have to work together.

Such feelings might have been prevented if all the participants in the selection procedure had been offered some kind of training in accordance with the results of the assessment centre; more emphasis should have been placed upon the development and opportunities available to all instead of upon limited selection for a very specific programme. The orientation of such a procedure should be towards possible alternatives being available for everyone depending on their qualities and interests. The outcome could be a certain kind of training for one person, an extensive course for another and, for yet another, promotion sooner or later depending also on other results being achieved in courses or on work assignments.

Remarkable side-effect: high goal-orientation

Perhaps the best testimonies to the procedure came from trainers who were not involved in the assessment centre. As is often the case, the trainers asked the trainees to formulate their own goals at the beginning of a training course. One experienced trainer stated:

These young employees, all under 25 years of age, appeared to be perfectly able to formulate precisely their goals and to operationalize them into specific training experiences. They had a sharp eye on their abilities and brought these well in line with possibilities and limitations of training situations. Working during a whole week with this group, I observed them reformulating and adapting their personal goals, depending upon their foregoing experiences. Among Dutch students and trainees I had never observed this before to such a high degree, as well as the ease and the realistic way in which they could talk about their own experiences—and failures!

For trainers and trainees this attitude, which was very likely to have been strongly influenced—or triggered off—by the assessment centre, made working with this group very rewarding.

Peer assessment and self-assessment

Not only were the trainees' goals adapted regularly, but new goals were also added. The trainees were discussing their own and their peers' experiences more frequently than was usual, especially in relation to their publicly formulated learning goals. Having experienced the assessment event may possibly have enabled this group to develop to a higher maturity and a more open learning attitude. This seemed to be a real support for further learning and growing.

Success story

Was the organization very short of supervisors and did the extra publicity given to the programme (because of its special character) influence people or was the programme really a success? The fact was that departments were already recruiting the participants long before the end of the programme. This, of course, was very encouraging to the participants, and not only served to free them from the fear of failure but was also very stimulating and encouraging. It must be recognized, however, that this may also have been partly a kind of self-fulfilling prophecy! At least we can say that all candidates succeeded and there were no drop-outs. The following year the programme was repeated successfully for a new group.

Assessment centres for outside candidates

After this first positive experiment the organization was open to the idea of further experiences with assessment centres. This time, the personnel department and all those responsible for recruitment and selection were enabled to be trained in order to apply the same techniques to the selection of candidates from outside the organization. Complete assessment centres were required for only very few outside candidates, but this new tool aroused curiosity among personnel managers (and some other managers as well) who wanted to know more about this powerful instrument. Many elements from the assessment training seminar proved to be useful not only for recruitment, selection and training but also for defining jobs and for appraisal and career development interviews. If you can observe someone who is already doing the target job you should not need simulations, but managers should be well trained in assessment and it may need an assessment centre to achieve that! In this case the training in assessment methods combined with appraisal interview training was made obligatory from top management down.

Success before the start

Assessment centres became very popular and in high demand throughout the organization. This was possibly because of positive feedback within the organization from the above-mentioned experiment and reinforced by the reactions from the first assessment centre training seminar for staff members from some personnel departments involved in recruitment and selection. The demand for training became too high at a certain stage. The outside consultants contracted to deliver these seminars and to implement this approach into the organization became almost overloaded and had to delay the provision of these seminars. Participation had to be limited to those staff members who could prove that they needed it for their selection and job appraisal activities.

Success has its limits ...

There was another side to this training demand as the limitation of participation aroused resistance and suspicion among lower levels of staff that management were being supplied with 'secret' instruments. This had to be quickly dealt with by an additional information-giving campaign to reassure people and this was followed by an agreement that additional adapted training for lower levels would be given. This proved a useful way of gaining acceptance for wider use of this approach.

Assessment centres became in a remarkably short time quite popular and were given a very positive rating throughout the organization.

This made it easier to use the same kind of methodology in improving other human resource systems in the organization, such as job evaluation, performance appraisal and career development. This was not always easy in an organization based on civil servants who had many years of experience and who had been accustomed for many years to stick to the rules which were formulated for eternity—or at least for a very long time!

Key points from the three cases

Why was the assessment centre method used?

The requirement in the German case was for new employees to fit with the 'lean production' philosophy, needing a specific attitude and social competence (e.g. teamwork) in addition to manual skills, for which an assessment centre was suited.

In the British case the need for more people to be identified as capable of development to distribution manager could not be met by existing appraisal and promotion methods. The assessment centre method was able to identify those with potential for development.

A total change of approach to work was needed in the Dutch case towards a competitive goal orientation from a government service attitude. The assessment centre was able to detect the potential to make this change.

What were the special benefits achieved by the method?

After both the pre-selection and selection stages feedback was given to participants in the German case enabling them to learn the attitudes and expectations of the company before they came together in the new factory. Two thousand new employees were selected and were successful in starting up the factory.

Special training in giving feedback and developing participants was given in the British case to the assessors who included two senior line managers; thus development was carefully integrated with assessment.

In the Dutch case the feedback made available to the participants enabled them to take considerable responsibility for their own learning in the training programmes which followed the assessment centre. The benefit from this was noted widely and helped to generate interest in using the method for other purposes.

What expertise was needed to deliver the benefits?

The company in the German case had the expertise to define its requirements and expectations from future employees according to a consistent set of values. The consultants had the expertise to analyse these and turn them into specific criteria which were used to design suitable exercises. They also had the ability to handle 10 000 applicants in a professional manner, including giving feedback to each participant in the assessment centre.

The regional managers in the British case had the expertise to predict future needs and identify a shortfall in the supply of ready-made distribution managers. The consultant had a method of defining the demands of the target role and designing exercises which specially suited the criteria. The training given to the four assessors (including two line managers) was able to equip them to carry out the feedback and development discussions which were needed to stimulate the full benefit.

In the Dutch case attention was given to encouraging everyone who was interested to come forward and participate in the selection and possible training programme. The feedback and information given to these young candidates were handled in such a way that participants took major responsibility for their future development.

What training did it depend on?

Certain principles in the German case were fundamental to the company's success in setting up the factory: among these were continuous improvement, quality and teamwork. As the consultants were acting on behalf of the company until production started, the project was highly dependent on the skill of the consultants in setting up valid and reliable assessment.

In the British case the observers/assessors had not carried out this work before so the training given to them before the assessment centres were run was crucial. Since the assessors also implemented the feedback away from the location of the assessment centre the training they had received on handling the feedback process was important for success.

There was a considerable shift in culture involved in the Dutch case, and various methods were needed to ensure that the participants, and other people around them, were fully aware of the project and its implications. Anxieties and suspicion had to be carefully handled, needing extra training and publicity at one point.

What development did the participants gain?

Through the feedback, in the German case, given after both the pre-selection and the selection events the participants learned where their weak points were and what kind of general attitude would be expected when they started work. The emotional investment made through participating in an assessment centre provides a basis for linking reflections with the experience.

The participants in the British case already worked within the company, but the assessment centre stretched them in ways beyond their current jobs. As they were given feedback on how they had been observed in such demands they were able to plan for their development through their work and through other means—one person out of 16 assessed was found to match the profile almost exactly and was very soon promoted to learn from the reality of doing the job. Others had their development guided by their regional managers.

In the Dutch case, those who were successful in gaining admittance to the one-year development programme were enabled to apply the feedback to the learning during the programme, which they did successfully. Those who did not gain admittance did not gain support for their development, and the organizers learned that this was a mistake: all participants should be offered development opportunities and support.

What development did the observers/ assessors gain?

In the German case much of the assessment work had to be done by the consultants who found the project stimulating and it provided new learning for them. One disadvantage of outsourcing is that much of the learning stays with the consultants and is not added to the company. In the process, however, the consultants got to know the company so well that they became much better prepared for new tasks which might arise in the same company in the future. This especially applies for international companies with a common philosophy valid for all the company's branches worldwide and where the consultants offer an international service.

The observers/assessors in the British case were highly involved in the assessment centre and in the feedback and development activities, and learned from this. The initial diagnostic work in establishing the criteria was carried out by the consultant so the development from doing this was not retained within the company.

In the Dutch case there was high involvement by many people in the organization in the assessment and development stages and in making the methods widely known in the company. The company was thus able to gain fully from the experience and the process assisted the attitude change needed in the transition to a competitive goal-oriented organization.

References and further reading

Anstey, E. (1989) 'Reminiscences of a Wartime Army Psychologist', *The Psychologist*, November 1989, 475–478.

Bolton, G.M. (1986) *Defining Managers' Jobs and Careers*, Roffey Park Institute, Horsham.

Coelius, C. (1992) *Fit fürs Assessment Center*, CC-Verlag, Hamburg.

Gijswijt, J. (1993) 'Assesseren als instrument voor loopbaangesprekken en voor MD on the job', *MD Journaal, Tijdschrift voor Management Development*, December, 22–24.

Kelly, G.A. (1955) *The Psychology of Personal Constructs*, Norton, New York (republished by Routledge, London, 1991).

Neuberger, O. (1990) *Führen und geführt werden*, Enke Verlag, Stuttgart.
Woodruffe, C. (1990) *Assessment Centres: identifying and developing competence*,
  Institute of Personnel Management, London.

3 Assessment within human resource development

Victor Ernoult

Introduction

The aim of this chapter is to show how assessment centres can be used as a management tool within the framework of a total human resources strategy. This of course implies that management, with the help of personnel directors, have considered their values and are clear about the main objectives they wish to achieve.

If used in the context of such discussions as a philosophy and total method of approach, assessment centres can become a very important driving force in the realization of business strategy.

Assessment centres operate in the field of 'behaviour', that is to say, there is an element open to change which can be shaped and improved and which facilitates development. Such behaviour, which is a response to stimuli drawn from work situations, is the subject of feedback from the observers in 'in vitro' situations (i.e. in an artificial environment), and from senior staff themselves in 'in vivo' situations (i.e. in the real environment).

In order to develop the assessment centre methodology into a more total human resources tool, it is simply moved from the narrow framework of evaluating potential and applied to other areas of human resources:

- job descriptions
- interviews and methods of performance appraisal
- a tool to identify training needs
- information sessions on jobs and required functions
- self-selection
- training for improved performance and coaching.

We will take two specific applications of this approach:

- fact-finding performance review
- use of assessment centres for vocational assessment and, in France, in the framework of the 'Bilan de Compétences' (the profiling, or 'balance', of competences).

This chapter will also examine the assessment centre approach in the context of 'in vivo' operations: essentially in the work situation the discovery of potential and coaching for career development.

The aim is to encourage the reader to consider the potential of a total human resources approach in which the various players involved use consistent tools in order to attain common goals.

Analysis of demands and of resistance to change

In planning a project the values and objectives of a company should be defined in an effort to identify its culture. From this, certain performance criteria can be established at the various levels of the organization. Working from the 'stimuli' arising from the business and working environment to arrive at the expected responses, behaviours, requirements and skills which underlie those criteria is to have a total and coherent approach. By virtue of its openness this allows candidates to understand how they are assessed and how they will be assessed in future jobs, and therefore this enables them to prepare.

Sociologists and psychologists have shown the need to overcome resistance to change in order to allow development.

Analysis of demands

This demand comes from three essential players:

1 The management
2 Personnel managers
3 The candidates.

The management

The most demanding management are generally found in the most open and innovative companies. The process implies that they will take part in these assessments, departing from the idea that identifying potential is for specialists only. Because of the clarity of objectives and means in this method they are able to enter the process easily. The relative simplicity of the method makes it accessible to non-specialists.

Dependence on personnel experts disappears. Whatever the initial training or educational background of the observer/assessor, it is possible to train him or her in just a few days.

Personnel managers

The role of personnel managers and consultants does not disappear as they are needed to monitor the process and train the observers/assessors.

The candidates

When confronted with this method, the candidates are aware of the relationship between what they are asked to do and the position applied for. It is striking that their own evaluation of their performance is very close to that of the observer/assessors. The determining factor in this approach is that it allows a dynamic dialogue between the three partners: candidate, management, specialists.

**Analysis of
resistance to
overcome when
implementing an
assessment centre
approach**

If a company does not have the will to take forward-looking steps there is little chance that assessment centres can be successfully implemented.

Cultural resistance

Business culture comprises a system of shared meanings. The management at the heart of the business is dependent on its technological and cultural 'givens': it moulds the mentality of managers and staff alike. For example, in France, sociologists such as Michel Crozier, Jean-Pierre Gruère and Thierry D'Iribarne have underlined the cultural characteristics which they see as essential to the French mentality.

Michel Crozier emphasizes the fear of dependent relationships, the fear of the abuse of power and an absolutist representation of authority. The American sociologist Laurence Wylie had already put forward the theory that the French educational system socialized children at an early age so that they accept authority without discussion. During adolescence, they seek to liberate themselves from prohibitions which young people strive to avoid: the individual hesitates between rebellion and submission to the system. The fear of being manipulated and the fear of 'being had' remains a cultural trait and a prevailing attitude to the first professional job. This defiance is accompanied by admiration for the charismatic and successful figures of authority, who are equally feared.

Jess Pitts notes that in France no authority can hope to be respected by the sole virtue of its functional authority or its hierarchical status. According to him, authority must demonstrate ownership of 'the magic of words and prove its superiority'; 'the baiting by French schoolchildren is a kind of embryonic revolution which implores authority to be dazzling'.

In order to escape this all-powerful authority of an administration focused around its top, procedural, restrained by promotion and seniority, divided into a layered hierarchy where qualifications dominate, managers depersonalize their dependence and short-circuit the hierarchical echelons. This fascination with the hallmarks of successful authority is mingled with a critical watchfulness for every sign of weakness.

These cultural tendencies are not particularly favourable to implementing managerial methods originating from and developed in an Anglo-Saxon context. However, by understanding this context, one can risk modifying traditional reactions which stem from the 'authoritarian' Latin education. Aspects of change are negotiated through dialogue between organizations and individuals. Some of these issues are discussed in more detail in the middle part of Chapter 4.

The implementation of an open and manageable human resources policy is achieved with the help of a training consultant who evaluates the organization's costs and investments, defines the measurable results and assesses in a positive fashion the necessary qualities to achieve these results.

Organizational resistance   Forward-looking personnel management is still strongly constrained by the reluctance of those responsible to sort and pass on relevant information. Human resources all too often remains a sacred and secret reserve.

The assessment of behaviour at different times in the life of an organization and in the life of a member of staff evidently poses risks of arbitration and confrontation.

A graphic representation of two key variables—classification and dissemination of knowledge—produces a typology of organizations (Boisot, 1982) which are at various stages in the management of human resources (Figure 3.1).

Four typical zones emerge, dependent on (a) whether or not information in the organization is sorted and classified, and (b) whether or not information is disseminated:

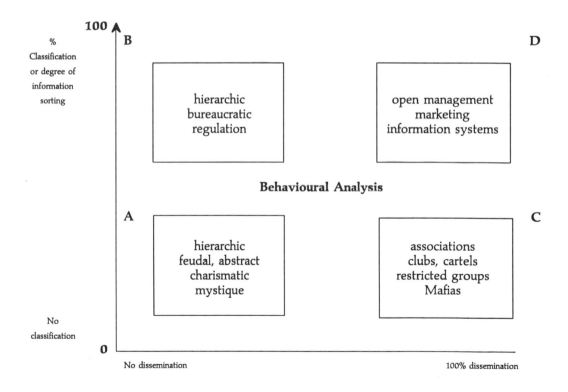

Figure 3.1   *The Max Boisot grid*

In zone A, where useful information is neither classified nor disseminated, the analysis of human resources is condemned to secrecy. The 'know-how' and the qualities of leadership remain inaccessible to un-initiated outsiders. Progress is made by a long and mysterious initiation: by word of mouth, by imitation and by immersion in hierarchical traditions.

In zone B, where information is classified but not disseminated, organizations are found where knowledge is the subject of exhaustive classification. Gone, however, are the directions for use, the manuals, the written rules, the index. Instead the information is often caught in the trap of bureaucracy which blocks it, holds on to it and uses it to strategic advantage. The absence of dissemination can be dictated by economic interests.

In zone C, where there is effectively no classification of information but much dissemination, amateur users of confidential and informal information are to be found. Associations and clubs take advantage of the spread of unsorted information which is not available in standardized form. Information is passed to restricted groups of sympathizers or partisans.

Zone D represents organizations where useful knowledge is both classified and disseminated. Its use is dictated by market culture. Openness is total and immediate, and information circulates at will on a supply and demand basis.

The success of assessment centre methods will depend on which of these four categories the organization matches.

In zone A organizations, it is difficult to establish an assessment centre approach. Management is too autocratic and any move towards classification or dissemination of information may be considered a loss of power. Assessment centred on behaviour would be contradictory to the rest of the system which is dominated by mistrust.

In zone B organizations, assessment centres will come into conflict with regulations. The absence of precise objectives and quantifiable results makes it almost impossible to identify criteria necessary for success.

In zone C organizations, there will be some difficulty in clarifying job definitions and establishing the requisite qualities as the practice is not to document or classify. This absence of reference material constitutes a major obstacle to openness.

The organizations in zone D obviously offer the most fertile ground for assessment centres. Here they will be used to the full because they fall into the category, as does the management in general, which allows classification and dissemination of useful information in terms of objectives, methods, results and evaluation. The culture of these organizations gives full support to forward-looking management and to assessment centres in particular.

In most of the countries in which we have had experience of assessment centres, we have discovered that organizations form a living history of industry. Many of them are still in zone A. Attempts at evolution have led in various directions: to zones B and C; or directly to zone D without necessarily passing through B or C as transitional phases.

What is perhaps more important than correctly diagnosing the zone in which an organization is located is to be able to identify and contrast the working methods of different departments within the same organization.

The need for individual responsibility

The nineties have highlighted the difficulties in forward-looking management, while at the same time it has become even more imperative that it should succeed. The reasons suggested are mistakes made in the past in forward planning and the need for a return to individual responsibility. It is to this that human resources specialists are responding while it is evident that forward-looking management is not made up of one project but of several projects which themselves have several scenarios. The return to the individual is not a surprise: career management can only be achieved when uniting the interests of both partners. One of the most healthy attitudes is to allow the individual to manage his or her own career; however, it will still be necessary to help in this process. The context of continuing crisis to some extent sets the record straight. The individual must be at the centre of his or her career and be the player. On the other hand, the best performing organizations seem to be those who are the most 'citizen-oriented', by giving their employees the means to manage themselves in this mobility and turbulence: going beyond the tools of outplacement, for example, the concept of 'employability' seems especially interesting. It consists in maintaining employees at a maximum performance level so that they are attractive to the employment market at all times.

In both cases, assessment centres are a tool which, through the feedback which is possible, helps to make those who benefit from it 'attractive'.

Specific resistance to assessment centres

Resistance to forward-looking personnel management is the real restraining factor to the assessment centre approach. In addition, there are specific areas of resistance to these methods which are often just excuses: with a little imagination it is possible to overcome them.

The time necessary, the price and the burden of the process are sometimes put forward as obstacles. This is only true of organizations which still remain closed to more participative methods of management. It indicates that preparatory work on the organization and mentality is necessary beyond the strict framework of setting up the assessment centre approach. In fact, the problem of cost is usually an excuse or disguises a belief in 'magic' solutions. The only answer for the consultant or the human resources manager is to show that assessment centres are an investment and not a cost.

Other resistance can arise from the fact that assessment centres are not infallible. Here the problem is not whether the method is perfect, but rather whether it is better than the alternatives. Evidence from various countries now points to the comparatively high validity of the kind of situational tests used in assessment centres.

Evolution of theories of people at work

General thoughts

The different movements which have sought to throw light on the dynamics of people at work serve as a reference to practitioners. It is therefore interesting to see how the various theories are compatible with the introduction of the assessment centre approach.

The economic debate

From Taylor to Drucker it has been the dominant theme. One can see the major interest in the performance cult, in the 'maximization of profit', a reality which is the most readily accountable—and often the only one—in the organization. This aspect remains as important as the crisis in which we find ourselves. Those who oppose this argument underline its only partial truth.

Internal and external causality

Another means of understanding the evolution of organizational theory is to emphasize the shift from the attribution of internal causality to external causality. It is a question initially of knowing how to organize the business, allocate resources, structure departments and assign personnel.

The vital importance of the organization in its environment is then underlined: it is beyond its immediate surroundings that the destiny of the organization is played out. The evolution of the total environment takes precedence over the internal rules of operation.

From Taylor to Herzberg

A third school of thought opposes the theories of the organization of work (Taylor): this is the discoveries in the human relations movement (Mayo) endorsed by the participationist movement (Maslow, McGregor, Herzberg, Likert). To Theory X, a pessimistic vision of people at work, McGregor opposes Theory Y, an optimistic vision which emphasizes the intrinsic interest that a person brings to work, the desire to manage oneself and to seek out responsibilities, as well as the ability to resolve problems encountered creatively.

Morse and Lorsch (1970) oppose this theory, refuting the idea that a universal structure of motivation exists and rejecting the concept of an ideal way of structuring and organizing an organization. The ideal way of organizing varies according to the activities and the people who lead them.

Business process re-engineering

Situational and environmental factors are becoming increasingly the determining factors in current thought. Belief in Taylorian systems has been demolished.

In view of the difficulties, new management methods try to stimulate innovation in order to confront, adapt, reconstruct the tasks, make bureaucracy more flexible. At first it was simply a question of limited improvements to traditional functions. From 1960 to 1975 qualitatively different innovations appeared, destined to increase efficiency and the capacity to absorb uncertainty: enriching jobs, semi-autonomous groups, participative management by objectives. These innovations demanded a consensus and an increasing level of participation.

Since 1975, the response to successive crises seems to have been the frantic search for adaptability to turbulence. A strategic analysis enables us to identify steps taken: return to seasonal forms of industry, dispersion of production activities, use of flexibility provided by sub-contracting, implantation in other regions of the world, managers' time shared between different organizations.

In this context, one of the latest movements in the study of people at work, the most enlightening, is that of business process re-engineering.

Jean-Pierre Gruère (1992) summarizes these four organizational theories around the diagram shown in Figure 3.2.

Influence of theoretical trends on the assessment centre approach

The upheavals in the business environment have encouraged organizational specialists to modify or reformulate their theories. The influence of these trends will have an immediate effect on the choice, definition and priority of criteria, dimensions and abilities retained. They reformulate the concept of man (humankind) and the underlying managerial model.

For several years therefore, the role played by criteria relating to external relations has been much greater. With increasing European and international activity, local characteristics and cultural differences must be taken into account. The national culture of the parent company will obviously be dominant, but as well as knowledge of the local language, communication criteria are even more important and cross-cultural sensitivity is essential for success in an international environment.

Jean-Pierre Gruère and Pierre Morel (1990) have used results from a major study of French managers who have worked abroad to construct a typology to assist with definition and evaluation in this cross-cultural work. According to them, the behaviour of managers falls into six main categories:

1 The cross-culturally handicapped
2 Partial amnesiacs
3 The blasé
4 The blocked

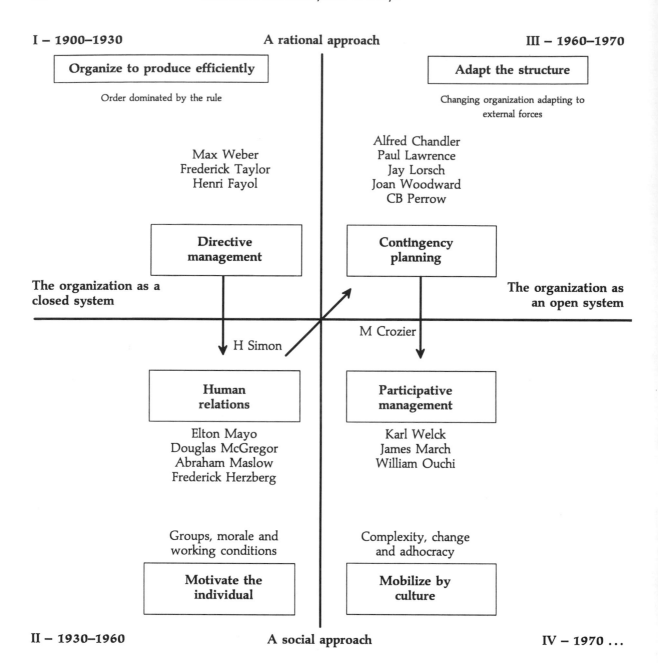

Figure 3.2 *Evolution of theories of the organization*

5 The converted
6 The clear-sighted, who demonstrate the highest cross-cultural sensitivity.

It might be interesting for those keen to develop and detect cross-culturalism to combine this typology with that of Thierry Gaudillot and Thomas Kamm (1990), which draws on a study of the chairmen of major French companies. They define four types of attitude:

1 The Euro-enthusiast
2 The Euro-vigilant
3 The Euro-serene
4 The Euro-transparent.

These two typologies are displayed in matrix form in Table 3.1 so that they can be contrasted, and possible links, causes and effects hypothesized.

Because the different theoretical trends influence managerial concepts, they also influence the choice and prioritization of criteria at the various levels of the organization. The first step is to make a diagnosis of the organization where the assessment centre is to be introduced. Where conditions are not sufficiently favourable, its use will be limited and will possibly lead to invalid results.

In some cases, its introduction may be a catalyst for a proactive investigation of the problems concerning assessment and for clarification of the management model.

The best climate is obviously that found in Max Boisot's zone D or in type IV described by Jean-Pierre Gruère: 'Mobilize by culture'.

Table 3.1 *Managers in Europe: two typologies of French managers*

	Attitude towards Europe			
Intercultural dimension	*Enthusiast*	*Vigilant*	*Serene*	*Transparent*
1. Handicapped				
2. Amnesic				
3. Clear-sighted				
4. Blasé				
5. Blocked				
6. Converted				

Can a Taylorian organization assimilate an assessment centre approach?

Is it possible for an organization whose managerial practice remains close to Taylorism to assimilate an assessment centre? The division between the conception and execution of work and the resulting centralization would render assessment centre practice unmanageable as it relies on participative management, transparency and feedback.

The knowledge and experience of the various 'players' in an assessment centre process have a place only in so far as it is possible to break down barriers. This concept of power-sharing, as described by Michel Crozier, makes it incompatible with the Taylorian model.

Bureaucracy and the assessment centre

Bureaucratic models are also unfavourable to the assessment centre approach. These organizations attach great importance to defining objectives, control and rationality. However, equally, interpersonal relations are devalued and considered irrelevant, with a corresponding loss of spontaneity and initiative. In more 'open' systems, the mobility of interpersonal relationships is one of the key factors which releases energy.

In the bureaucratic model, the blockage is caused by staff dissatisfaction faced with the demands of management control, the importance given to form, regularity of behaviour and expected uniformity. There is little flexibility, with no possible variation in response to environmental demands.

As one of the basic principles of the approach is goal congruence and a negotiated agreement on the necessary requirements for success, the assessment centre cannot develop in a bureaucratic context. This does not mean that such organizations who wish to use the assessment centre as a tool to effect change need be excluded. There are many examples where French companies have successfully transformed their management practice in this way.

Participationism, the contingency theory and the assessment centre

Organizations influenced by the 'participationist' or 'contingency' schools of thought are those most likely to receive maximum benefit from the assessment centre approach. Morse and Lorsch (1970) sum up these ideologies in emphasizing that the key is to succeed in matching task–organization–personnel. Keeping the goals in mind, they underline the energy generated when the organization transforms itself to adapt both to the task and the staff. This is the heart of the assessment centre approach which, by identifying the working practices of staff and at the same time adapting its own methods, achieves the best. Stimuli and simulated working situations allow for problem solving without predetermining a precise answer. In principle, the approach avoids reproducing identical results and thereby giving value to clones. It allows the integration of original profiles and the development of atypical talent by admitting them into the hierarchy. The contingency movement seems to reduce effectively the risk of worldliness or excessive idealism present in participationist thought. In a difficult economic context, the idea of competition and the battle to defend one's business and job become pre-eminent.

The assessment centre approach as a pivot for forward-looking management

Forward-looking personnel management can only thrive within the larger framework of organizational management. If the organization defines its targets, the human resources are able to offer their support. Crises, hazards and the fact that forecasts may prove to be wrong will not change anything. The difficulties in a task do not prove right those who wish to kill it off.

On the other hand, this period of greater realism will certainly eliminate many of the career management systems which become overly sophisticated in attempting to 'model-make' excessively, thereby becoming 'hot air machines'.

It would be very disturbing for an organization to return to navigation by sight when, according to Pierre Jardillier (1982), we are already used to instrument navigation, simply on the pretext of excess. No-one has ever become a doctor or an engineer without having made a plan or at least accepted one, which has not prevented others from changing course. Without making an absolute rule, experience has shown that five-year plans are sufficiently motivating for employees.

Assessment centres are strong tools for forward-looking management because they ensure that it passes from theory to practice by confronting staff with their future responsibilities or anticipating them by 'in vitro' situations which allow observation. They are therefore directed to career paths, development plans and promotion. Assessment centres permit the move from a quantitative and probabilist approach to an individual 'nominative' approach which answers two questions:

- Who is able to respond to the requirements of new functions (detection)?
- How can we be prepared for these changes (career development, training, coaching)?

Various possible applications of assessment centres: the relevance of a total assessment centre approach

Other chapters of this book have illustrated how assessment centres can play a part at various times in an individual's career, as shown in Table 3.2.

At these different stages in an employee's life, the assessment centre method may be used in the orthodox sense as a simulated situation which allows 'in vitro' observation in a controlled environment. The principle is maintained for this of concentrating on the crucial elements of the process, which are:

- representative critical incidents
- the behaviours which they elicit
- dimensions and abilities revealed.

These are developed, from assessment centre methods, by using more 'targeted' tools without putting employees in an artificial situation by using the following:

- the job description inspired by the assessment centre approach
- the fact-finding interview during recruitment or appraisals
- the career questionnaire and career interview for a vocational assessment, which allows the individual to build a career plan
- the career plan questionnaire, which helps the candidate, who is putting together the plan, to identify critical incidents—and the skills required to deal with them—involving those who hold similar responsibilities to those the candidate wishes to achieve.

The following are still to be developed according to the same 'philosophy':

- a reference system for the 'careers in organizations' committees who

Table 3.2   *Times in a career when assessment centres can be used*

Evaluation and recognition of potential	
	• Recruitment
	• Transfer
	• Promotion
	• Redirection (including outplacement)

can also draw on behavioural observations in real situations
- 'in vivo' placements, both to discover and develop potential. This happens already in 'coaching' situations.

Actual placement to discover potential has not yet been used sufficiently. It poses methodological problems in guaranteeing reliability. However, it is possible to compensate for the subjectivity of a single observer or the time discrepancy in observations, or the indirect evaluation of results, by increasing the number of observers and placements.

This 'in vivo' approach can offer an interesting alternative in cases where an 'in vitro' approach is not appropriate.

These various stages of possible application of the assessment centre approach are summarized in Figure 3.3.

'360° appraisals'

More recently developed, 360° appraisals involve a manager asking a member of staff and others from the working team to provide an appraisal which is then compared to his or her own self-assessment.

This method takes the idea from the assessment centre of focusing on the relevant criteria. It is also based on behaviour observed during encounters with the job holder set up in response to stimuli (the critical incidents which he or she has to deal with).

The employee's network of relationships

As can be seen from Figure 3.4, the aim is to have feedback from at least one assessor at each functional level, drawn from the people who come into contact with the job holder.

As shown in the diagram, the information obtained is not limited to the internal network but includes, for example, a client satisfaction index. It highlights employees who have strong customer service skills. Each person is able to improve weak areas by setting objectives and receiving feedback.

The business plan and appraisals

When an organization decides to form a business plan, it must establish its values, set the objectives and, as a result, the criteria for measuring the performance of its staff, at all functional levels, will emerge. The principal role in this for human resource specialists is to maintain coherence between the organization's strategic objectives and the criteria used to assess the performance of each job holder.

Conclusion

The assessment centre and future perspectives

Future perspectives for this approach are linked to its ability to adapt to actual situations and to maintain its forward-looking direction.

Key stages in the assessment centre approach

Job description

Critical incidents
Individual situations, one-to-one and group (%)
Criteria and abilities needed

Recruitment

Fact-finding interview
Identify candidate's behaviour
Evaluation in relation to the criteria and abilities needed in the job envisaged

Assessment centre 'in vitro'
Simulations
Use of observers

Evaluation of performance

Management observation on behaviour demonstrated in critical situations,
results obtained, skills demonstrated
Feedback and exchange with the staff member during the appraisal interview
based on:
- observed behaviour
- skills needed

Defining new objectives
Plan to improve required skills

Identifying potential

Tasks focusing on 'in vivo' observation relating to the criteria required in
the job sought
Put into 'in vitro' situations: simulations (best-known use of the
assessment centre)
Put into a succession of 'in vivo' situations (several situations, different
observers, evaluation of results in relation to the criteria)

Development of potential

Assessment centre sessions 'in vitro' used again to develop performance
areas seen to be weak
Use of results for training/coaching
A succession of 'in vivo' placements to develop areas of performance

Figure 3.3 *Key stages in the assessment centre approach*

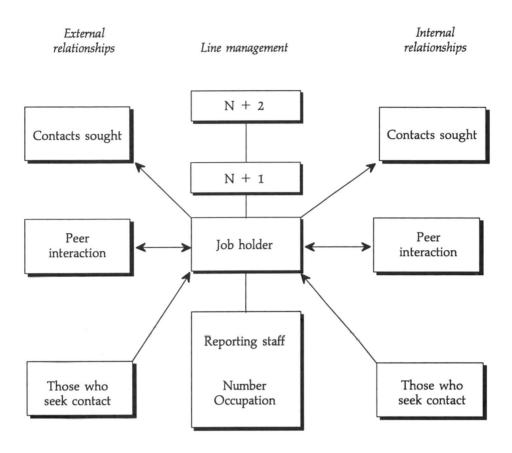

Figure 3.4 *The network of relationships*

The economy demands that theoretical models be constantly updated. In recent years models have evolved to take account of downsizing and the need of many organizations to cut back.

Assessment centres have had to adapt to these new contexts. Their organization and increasing international use have also led to a refocusing on the ability of staff to assimilate this new factor.

Although during the past 20 years the assessment centre has largely developed in a business environment, its sphere of influence has spread to higher education; in particular, management colleges and, more recently, government organizations have become more open to these methods.

Finally, in France, we should mention the 'Bilan de Compétences' (i.e. a kind of profiling of competences). Since 1992 each employee may request an external 'check up' by a public or private body. Assessment centres will have an essential role to play among the suggested tools.

References and further reading

Boisot, M. (1982) 'The Culture of the Firm: the Japanese Enterprise in its International Environment', Document de Travail 82–18, Groupe ESCP, Paris.

Crozier, M. (1963) *Le Phénomène Bureaucratique*, Seuil, Paris.

Crozier, M. (1970) *La Société Bloquée*, Seuil, Paris.

D'Iribarne, T. (1989) *La Logique de l'Honneur*, Seuil, Paris.

Gaudillot, T. and Kamm, T. (1990) *Mille jours pour réussir l'Europe*, Editions Jean-Claude Lattes, Paris.

Gruère, J-P. (1992) *Ouvrage Management, aspects humains et organisationnels*, Presses Universitaires de France, Paris.

Gruère, J-P. and Morel, P. (1990) *Cadres français et Communications interculturelles*, Eyrolles, Paris.

Herzberg, F. (1968) *Work and the Nature of Man*, Staples Press, London.

Jardillier, P. (1982) *La Maîtrise de l'emploi*, Presses Universitaires de France, Paris.

Likert, R. (1961) *New Patterns of Management*, McGraw-Hill, New York.

Maslow, A.H. (1970) *Motivation and Personality*, 2nd ed., Harper and Row, New York.

Mayo, E. (1933) *The Human Problems of an Industrial Civilization*, Macmillan, New York.

McGregor, D. (1960) *The Human Side of Enterprise*, McGraw-Hill, New York.

Morse, J.J. and Lorsch, J.W. (1970) 'Beyond Theory Y', *Harvard Business Review*, May/June, 61–68.

Pitts, J. (1964) *A la Recherche de la France*, Seuil, Paris.

Taylor, F.W. (1911) *Principles of Scientific Management*, Harper and Row, New York.

Wylie, L. (1970) *Chanzeau, Village d'Anjou*, Gallimard, Paris.

Wylie, L. (1979) *Un Village du Vaucluse*, Gallimard, Paris.

4 Differences across Europe

Mac Bolton, Jean-Luc Spriet, Jan Gijswijt, Hélio Moreira and Ulrike Hess

It is difficult to draw tight boundaries around parts of Europe and identify the characteristics of human resource methods that apply in any one part or country. A *perception*, however, is that the Latin countries take a warmer, more personal approach to assessment of people and that the Northern countries are more willing to be guided by analysis and numerical ratings. As an example of how the more analytical approach has been used to assess managers for senior international roles we give details of some aspects of an assessment centre designed for Ericsson, the international telecommunications manufacturer, whose head office is in Sweden. We go on to suggest how the Latin approach may provide a different way, in some respects, of going about assessment and development initiatives. The third part of the chapter provides interesting information on a contrast between the former East and West parts of Germany through the work that Ulrike Hess and her team at tpm have been doing in helping companies in both parts of Germany since 1990. We draw out some implications for projects in cross-cultural assessment and development at the end of the chapter.

The Northern analytical approach

Assessment for senior management

The project reported here was centred on Britain and on fairly senior managers based there at the time of the project. Several of the managers were Swedish and already had international experience. In developing the criteria used in the assessment centre the sample of senior managers who were consulted included five from Sweden who at the time were working in Britain. Thus within this project we are able to identify some differences between the Swedish and British senior managers in the priority order they gave when they were asked to rank the criteria, in addition to giving an example of an assessment centre that used an analytical approach.

The assessment centre was seen as the first step on a development path for people rising towards senior management positions. The process was planned to take the following course:

1 Identification of candidates who were seen to be possible potential senior managers and who were prepared to be considered for such development.
2 Assessment centre for assessment of the potential of these candidates for senior management roles.
3 An individualized development plan to prepare people for an international management role, which would be likely to include a spell of at least a few months in Sweden.

As the assessment centre would be held in Britain for mostly British managers it was agreed that the criteria and exercises used should be developed for a British cultural environment, though linking in with the Swedish/international criteria already in use for assessment and development purposes in Sweden and elsewhere.

The process of analysis and planning was as follows:

1 Individual interviews were held with all current senior managers in Britain using the 'repertory grid' approach whereby the behaviours of more effective and less effective managers were contrasted and the constructs of good performance were elicited (Bolton, 1986).
2 The information from the repertory grid interviews was clustered and integrated into 21 combined constructs and listed in random order giving full definitions but no headings.
3 The list of constructs was given to the 13 senior managers who had contributed towards them; they were then asked to rank them in order of importance for effective performance in senior management roles internationally in the company.
4 A link was made with the Swedish/international criteria to ensure that where possible there was compatibility and use of common definitions and forms of expression where this was achievable without distorting the data. The result was 14 criteria drawn from the interviews and two other criteria needed to complete the coverage of the Swedish criteria.

An example of one of these main criteria from the interviews that was then used in designing the assessment centre was the following:

Has a wide perspective and looks ahead, reading situations well and anticipating any potential problems rather than firefighting later. Has flexible attitudes, discusses new ideas and listens to different or opposing views, working with cross-fertilization of ideas to find solutions from a broader base, rather than being parochial.

The process of design then followed the pattern already described in Chapter 2 for the distribution manager project in Britain: a matrix of the 14 criteria against various exercises was drawn up so that most of the criteria were measured in at least three different ways. For instance, the criterion given above, which was labelled 'Perspective', was measured in a written exercise, in a leaderless group discussion, in an in-tray exercise which had several items that tested it, and through comparing these measurements with the score on one of the dimensions of a personality questionnaire. The exercises were all shaped to test the specific criteria being measured in this assessment centre rather than using 'off-the-shelf' ones.

The usual processes were then followed to ensure reliability of observation, including:

- allocation of observer roles so that each observer had a manageable load, spread across the various candidates in different exercises
- observers and role-players were trained so that they were performing consistently at the same standard as each other
- a trial of the various exercises was held and modifications made so that ambiguities were reduced and misunderstandings removed
- clear briefing, written and oral, was given to the candidates to ensure that they fully understood the purpose of the assessment centre and had a general appreciation of the criteria being measured.

The evaluation of the behaviours observed was carried out by bringing together all those who had been observers in the assessment centre so that the different perceptions and interpretations in senior management could be integrated to produce assessments that were as valid as possible for the Swedish/British culture of the UK parts of the company. The results from the assessments were discussed with the participants individually, and their aspirations and interests were fitted together with the assessments made of their potential, leading to individualized development plans.

Swedish/British comparison

Returning to Step 3 mentioned above, when the original list of 21 combined constructs was given to the 13 senior managers, it was possible to separate out the rank orders given by the Swedish managers from those given by the British managers. The sample of five Swedish managers and eight British is, of course, small, and general conclusions about differences in national cultures cannot be drawn; but the views of this group are well considered and based on their experience of management in Ericsson in the two countries. They are therefore worth investigating to see if they reveal a consistent difference which can be related to perceived style patterns experienced within the company.

The method of finding average rank orders for two or more groups of managers has been used to compare other kinds of differences in other organizations, for instance between technologists and general managers, and between accountants and administrators. These differences are always found to be based on reality and are confirmed by later investigations. There seems to be no reason therefore to disregard the trends that are described here.

Some of the 21 initial constructs did not produce identifiably different rank orders between the Swedish and British managers. For instance, the following were ranked much the same by both groups:

- looking ahead to anticipate problems and finding solutions from a broad base
- being able to manage upwards, understanding the person being reported to and offering information, but able to take action independently
- representing the interests of the organization, being professional without being influenced by pressures and prepared to stand up for beliefs
- understanding the result that should be achieved in any project, delivering it at the right time in the right way
- willing to work in other countries, learn other languages and express oneself in another culture
- encouraging women and ethnic minorities, taking account of their different needs so that there is a large pool of talent upon which the company can draw.

The Swedish managers ranked the following constructs as *considerably more important* than the British managers did:

- having the mental capacity and agility to handle simultaneous tasks and being able to switch rapidly without getting lost or confused
- being available to work whatever hours are necessary to see the job through or to travel, and contactable at any time to deal with problems rather than blocking contact.

In addition, they ranked the following as *slightly more important* than British managers did:

- planning and organizing work in a logical fashion, taking time to break down tasks and prioritize them, sorting out importance and urgency; able to cope with pressure
- being skilled in selecting staff and able to release responsibility, coaching and trusting staff to do the job, giving encouragement and feedback, identifying aspirations and development needs.

On the other hand, the British managers ranked the following constructs as *more important* than the Swedish managers did:

- skill in communicating with others in meetings of various kinds, resolving conflict constructively
- having a worldwide network of contacts within the company and taking the initiative in offering support to another part of the company.

In addition, they ranked the following as *slightly more important* than the Swedish managers did:

- monitoring performance against budget, putting forward realistic ideas on the business, reviewing activities to find improvements in quality
- being accessible to customers, putting them first and responding creatively to their needs
- wanting to improve and thinking about self-development; showing initiative in taking on more work and responsibility.

The significance of differences

Some of the differences between Swedish and British managers can be seen to be based on different circumstances in the two countries, although before seeing these results nobody predicted them. For example, as the British telecommunications industry was 'privatized' before other similar organizations in other countries of Europe, it is not surprising that British managers should have a more responsive attitude to customers and be more quality minded, particularly with British government pressure for compliance with BS 5750 standards or ISO 9000 internationally. Other differences could be debated as arising from different traditions in society or in assumptions about management style, and some of them are, in fact, in reasonable accord with differences between Swedish and British managers identified in a recent book on 'culturo-managerial' issues (Hill, 1994). Another point worth further investigation is that in a country where the head office of an international company is located there may be greater pressure on the mental faculties and time commitment of senior managers.

Whatever the actual differences, the principle is worth making explicit that there may well be philosophical, cultural and attitudinal differences between national groups within the same company as other researchers have shown (Hofstede, 1991). The analytical method outlined in the study reported here has shown itself to be capable of identifying some of these differences, which may be only short-lived and will need checking as circumstances change. These differences may indeed be healthy and can enable predictions to be made of how one country's attitudes may move towards another, for instance if a major change such as privatization spreads from one country to another.

The Latin approaches

It is, of course, making an assumption that one can group a few countries together and make some generalizations about them as if they share common characteristics. There are often attitudes from history that determine different patterns of thought and reaction, even though there may be geographical proximity and some shared linguistic patterns. Northern Europeans may assume that because Spain and Portugal share the same peninsula they have common approaches. Others may even assume that because Portugal is a long-standing ally and trading partner of Britain they share the same business and social priorities. Both assumptions could be badly wrong. Nevertheless, there are grounds for seeing if one can identify some common attitudes to the assessment of people between the 'Latin' countries of France, Italy, Spain and Portugal.

In this chapter we will especially study the situation in France and compare this, where possible, with the situation in the other countries mentioned.

Selection procedures in France

('Find me an excellent candidate!': 'For what?': 'We'll see')

As we know from Shackleton and Newell (1991), the number of assessment centres for selection purposes has been considerably smaller in France than in Britain. Some 58.9 per cent of the sample of British companies report using it, as opposed to 18.8 per cent in France. They found that its use in France is confined exclusively to organizations with more than 500 employees. What they did not measure, however, was the number of international companies in the sample based outside France compared with French-based companies, and whether any of the latter were applying assessment centres for selection purposes.

Around the same time, Bruchon-Schweitzer and Ferrieux (1991) published a survey on selection and recruitment in France taken among 60 consultants and 42 companies. This survey revealed clearly that recruitment in France had developed independently from the accumulated (mainly Anglo-Saxon) research. Among the methods used, after interviews, graphology scored second among consultants and third in national companies.

Surprisingly also, morpho-psychology (12 per cent of the consultants) and astrology (8.5 per cent of the consultants) were among the methods used. The authors mention in their conclusion the return to irrationality in companies which is not limited to recruitment but seems also to extend itself to investment decisions based on feeling or astrological data.

Yet the number of consultants offering assessment centre services is increasing considerably. It leaves us with the question: Where do they find their clients?

Training and development

At about the same time as the above-mentioned research was being carried out, some interesting assessment projects were taking place in France. For the 'Caisses d'Epargne Ecureuil', for instance, one of the most important savings banks in France, the Assessment Centre Department of Infraplan (now 'Optimhom') was charged with a challenging project. During the past two decades the bank had made an impressive change from a simple savings bank into an organization selling over 100 banking services and now exposed to the competition of many other professional financial institutions. This necessitated a new type of local agent ('Chef d'agence').

Turning to the future Hiring so many new people, of course, was out of the question. How could the agents from the past be helped to adapt to fit into the present and be prepared for the future? It was clear from the beginning that rather revolutionary new ways had to be developed.

As a first step, the agents themselves were invited to formulate what were, in their eyes, critical activities and fields of special attention in the actual execution of their function. The second step was a comparable question put to the next higher level, in combination with the question of what skills and behaviour were considered necessary for the agents to succeed.

The third step was taken to ensure that this analysis was well directed to the future working conditions of the agents. A strategic force formulated the new activities foreseen for the agents and the hierarchy of importance of emerging activities.

These steps led towards the formulation of necessary skills and competences, but also involved the people directly concerned and thus engaged them right from the start in this process of change. They were aware and were assured that they would obtain help and guidance in adapting themselves in their changing situation.

'Appreciation centres' preceded the individualized 'bilan' The assessment centres which followed were called 'Centres d'Appréciation des Compétences en Situation' (Centres for appreciation of situational competences), thus adding clearly positive meanings to the more neutral words 'assessment' and 'skills', but maybe at the same time 'Frenchifying' American methods. The exercises were situated not in a banking environment, but in a general service company.

The follow-up after the individual feedback sessions was, however, essential. The concrete, factual feedback in line with the whole evaluation made the participants aware step-by-step of their personal training needs. Fitting in with the previously formulated hierarchy of required competences a number of training possibilities could be offered in which people could participate according to their uncovered (and/or discovered) needs.

Education In France one's education is valued, and, if active in business, attendance at one of the leading educational institutes which are recognized in business is an important start to a career. The 'Grandes Ecoles' (a small number of the best higher education institutes) are the natural points of reference: only very few highly selected students qualify, and the limited number of graduates automatically belong to the intellectual elite. The intellectual training which this gives is distinctive, and it is not surprising that graduates from such a place are reassured when someone whom they are considering has had the identical *Grande Ecole* education to them. A meeting between such people can readily establish that there is a common framework of thought and that the natural assumption of compatibility will be achieved in practice. Thus an interview or a series of interviews involving all interested parties has been the traditional means of negotiating a place in a team or organization.

In Portugal the population is low compared with the larger countries of Europe, the number of higher education institutes is small (but growing), and career development is facilitated by the series of networks that are in existence among graduates of those universities and institutes. Throughout the Latin countries, of course, there are numerous employees who are not graduates and have not had significant experience of further education, but methods of assessment and development have been influenced by the experience of those who provide the intellectual lead in organizations.

Relationships

In contrast to the patterns of managing that stem from the intellectual training and theoretical frameworks shared by people in France and similar countries there is the important matter of relationships. It is seen as vital that a technical task does not exclude the building up of trust, correct courtesies and the recognition of the due worth of a particular person. Assessing a person solely in terms of ratings, numbers and a faceless total would not do justice to the warmth, humanity and creativity which that person can potentially bring to a group of people. Assessment centres and development centres do not, of course, exclude these attributes—indeed, they may be specifically measured—and yet the French (or Latin?) approach senses that there is still an indefinable something ('Je ne sais quoi!') which is identified as part of gradually developing a relationship leading to compatible roles.

This identification process is seen in action in preparing to do business between organizations or individuals. It may take several meetings, in some of which little business is discussed, before the parties are ready to move to a firm commitment. When that barrier has been overcome the business can be negotiated quite quickly, and it would be disappointing to both parties if, after the extensive preliminaries, a major obstacle was encountered. Similarly with people being assessed and developed, once a relationship has been established there is usually high commitment to follow through the process to ensure that it leads to productive careers and a cohesive team whose members show loyalty to each other.

Other cultural and psychological barriers to 'assessment'

As if the natural cultural and 'humanistic' barriers do not limit sufficiently the possibilities for assessment centres to prosper on French soil, recently the government added its much criticized so-called 'Law Toutbon' officially prohibiting all English terms from being taken over into the French language. This not only puts a fine on the word 'assessment', but more importantly illustrates the French struggle against the penetration of foreign words and influences.

This resistance has been felt, however, for many decades. No wonder

French psychologists call their assessment centre 'Le Bilan Comporte-mental'. (The word *Bilan* is of Latin/Italian origin, but has long been accepted/admitted in France.) As there now exist several expressions in this field, such as 'Bilan des capacités', it was no problem to establish the meaning of this word. A *bilan*, as everywhere in French society, is the instrument for obtaining a quantitative overview of the (financial) situation. It implies insight into the state of the organization and gives important information about strengths and weaknesses. It suggests and requires regular review and analyses for improvement.

Shifting the attention and emphasis from assessment towards *bilan* also takes away or weakens the 'judgement' character of the procedure, strengthening the emphasis on insight for improvement. Assessments are made first, the *bilan* comes later and activities for improvement follow. Placing the *bilan* in the middle changes the emphasis of the whole procedure.

Finally, the accent on the *bilan* aspects of the procedure may be linked with the increasingly emancipatory influences that we have seen in recent years. Assessments originated during the Second World War in the army, which generally is not considered the cradle of democratic procedures. Since the war emancipation has taken place everywhere, not least in the economically prosperous countries: it was precisely in these countries that assessment centres were expected to flourish, but that should not and could not be brought about by imposing these new methods upon increasingly perceptive organizational groups: By involving the groups in formulating requirements, composing the *bilan* and choosing alternatives, sources of resistance are likely to be overcome.

The creative French with their human resource *bilan* silently found an important concept through which this method could be better accepted and embraced by the people who can profit from it. At the same time we observe in the Anglo-Saxon world the 'invention' of peer assessment and self-assessment which may indicate developments in the same direction!

Compromises are needed

During the last ten years there has been increasing recognition, perhaps still by a minority of organizations, that it is possible to combine the more analytical approaches favoured by Northern European countries with the more 'human' style favoured by Latin countries. There are good reasons for this change, in that there is an appreciation that in the increasingly complex business scene some of the old assumptions may no longer be valid. New skills are needed, new approaches and a mix of various kinds of cultures. Existing professional networks may no longer be enough. The use of intellectually neat methods such as testing and graphology may not be identifying the new competences which are in demand, particularly as companies become more international in outlook and composition. Some leading commentators on methods used by human resource departments have recently been critical of some subjective and invalid methods of assessment. The debate is shifting from claiming theoretical sophistication to facing up to the results obtained from assessment and development in practice.

A recent example of this new approach is provided by Novotel, the French-based international hotel group. In conditions of difficult trading, senior management became convinced that the hotel managers worldwide could be helped to improve their performance and thus ensure that the group improved its results and the employees gained greater satisfaction in their careers. The first task was to generate reliable and valid information on the abilities needed to be an effective hotel manager in Novotel. The results of a study and discussions with senior management brought out four areas grouping the abilities needed:

1 *Conceptual*	• Perceptual	
	• Judgement	
	• Initiative	
2 *Application*	• Decision taking	
	• Implementation	
	• Organization and planning	
3 *Inspiring others*	• Leadership	
	• Delegation	
	• Follow-up and monitoring	
4 *Relating*	• Adaptability	
	• Interaction with people	
	• Written communication	
	• Oral communication	

As shown above, within each of these four areas there were three abilities (except for *Relating* which had four, to ensure that both written and oral communication were included). Each ability has five detailed criteria which allow for differentiating between behaviours which vary from a routine response to an in-depth creative achievement. This system of abilities is both intellectually rigorous and also demanding in a practical way that relates to results.

An assessment centre was designed to test all these abilities by means of a written in-tray exercise, three role-plays and a group discussion. The analysis of these results was found to be a considerable task, particularly in countries which had large numbers of hotel managers to develop, such as France and Britain. At this point the *compromise* was seen in that, although provision was made of a rating scale and numerical weightings for the assessors to use in a detailed analysis, the nature of the behaviours and the need to retain the motivation of the participants led to the grouping of performance on each ability into three broad categories. This enabled the bottom category to be identified as the 'threshold' performance, meaning that a hotel manager had at least achieved a starting level in the ability, but now needed fairly urgently to do some training and development work to raise performance to the level of one of the other two categories. An individual development plan was agreed jointly with hotel managers by their directors, and learning was seen as a positive activity to be engaged in, whichever of the three categories applied. Reports from the assessors were based on the scoring of behaviours on the criteria, but feedback discussions pointed towards the possibility of learning in a creative, supportive way through the programmes made available to participants.

Extension of the assessment centre to Portugal and Spain needed appropriate translation into each language and a few adjustments to suit employment legislation, but the philosophy and approach were consistent. For Britain, similarly, translation into English was needed and the case material was re-located to London, but some of the participants there were of French origin and it was important to retain the common approach and be sensitive to difficulties of language and differences between cultures represented. The English version of the assessment centre was also used in Canada and the USA and the compromise between the Northern need for analytical rigour and the Latin approach seemed to hold firm for all these countries, motivated by the commitment to respect the international nature of the company and its special strength in France. With goodwill, it seems from the ACE experience of working together on the Novotel project that these approaches can converge and produce helpful synergy.

An additional gain from the international aspect of this Novotel project, according to Evelyne Chabrot, Group Human Resource Manager for Novotel, is the improved possibility of planning and anticipating changes and movements of people.

Human resource development in France

From our point of view it was a pity that Shackleton and Newell (1991) limited their research to selection procedures. We expect—as we have illustrated—that for development uses of assessment centres the figures would be different. From our own recent experiences it seems likely that French companies are more open to apply assessments for human development.

As is known from what happened in France, as well as in some other countries in Europe, American companies took the lead in Europe in introducing assessment centres for selection purposes. After a very slow start, these methods were adopted and adapted by a small number of internationally-orientated large companies. Our recent experiences with non-American companies in this field suggest that if European companies include assessment centres it is rather for human resource development or for development and selection purposes together.

This may be even more so in the case of France, because more than 10 years ago the French government recognized the need for employees of all levels and educational backgrounds to enjoy the advantages of life-long continued education. Since that time a fixed percentage of personnel costs have to be reserved each year for training and further education. Since hardly any training tradition existed in many companies, educational activities had to be set up within a rather short period of time. This meant that in many cases there was a need to set up new structures and new professional schemes without much experience.

The disadvantage of this was that there was some disorder in the beginning, but the advantage was that there was plenty of space for new ideas and initiatives, unhindered by much baggage from the past. This has provided an opportunity for experimenting with new methods.

Developments in Italy

Although in literature on assessment centres in Italy (Shackleton and Newell, 1993) we do not find much information suggesting there are many such activities in Italy, a European survey on the assessment centre method presented in Venice (October 1992) may shed some additional light. The method was started in 1974 by Montedison for selection purposes, but more recently experience in 52 firms has been mainly in the field of evaluating potential for human resource development purposes. Also mentioned were new procedures or adapted instruments such as computerized self-assessment (for low-ranking positions) and self-assessments/personal interviews (for high-ranking positions). Although we lack sufficient detail about the Italian situation, nothing indicates, however, a development much different from that in France; on the contrary, the above-quoted figures and developments seem to match well.

Developments in Spain

The same survey mentions, for Spain, that General Motors was the first organization that set up and ran a company-wide assessment centre in the mid-seventies. There were two different assessment centres: one was set up to select and train 6000 unskilled workers, and the other to select 400 supervisors.

At the time of the survey not much information could be gathered in Spain, although some assessment centres were mentioned in the field of potential evaluation, for identification of training needs and for human resource development purposes. The high cost and the 'American look' were mentioned as the main restrictions. As the General Motors design was based on the organization's experiences in Oklahoma it may be that the further development of assessment centres in Spain could profit from a more human and (Latin?) European style as developed in France.

The low status of human resource management and the slower economic development, together with the lower number of big companies, may very well account for the low rate of use of assessment centres in Spain. Without further information, however, we are unable to put forward any hypotheses about the situation or suggest likely further development.

Developments in Portugal

We have already reported in Chapter 1 on the situation in Portugal and given some indications of the cultural and other reasons for the fairly recent changes taking place in assessment and development. The influence of Assessment Circle Europe has been of significance in some of the changes, drawing on wider European experience but finding solutions that match the local and topical need. In Chapter 5 a detailed Portuguese case is reported which shows how a new management approach to assessment and development took account of the prevailing culture and found an acceptable way forward in introducing new methods in a way that encouraged cooperation and recognized human values.

Conclusion

Comparing the Latin countries, we see that in France, Italy and Spain there was usually a line of introduction of assessment centres through one or more American companies in the seventies, though in the case of Portugal it was in the late eighties through British support of Portuguese consultants. Mostly this took place through a few large international organizations and sometimes through some of the biggest national ones such as banks, computer companies and service organizations.

Resistance against American and Anglo-Saxon influences in these countries may be stronger than in some other countries, but other resistance could be due to a feeling of 'being judged'. We have found adaptations suited to 'Latin' approaches which use ways and means of overcoming overt judgement. Other adaptations which have been indicated are in the direction of a more human or humanistic approach compared with the numerical, analytical Anglo-Saxon way. Applications in the field of human resource development may be more acceptable and more promising than in selection and recruitment.

Comparison of some experiences gained with the implementation of assessment centres in West Germany and East Germany during the period 1990–92

Since the political change in autumn 1989 people of former East Germany have been confronted with radical changes which have had tremendous effects in all fields. When looking at the previous methods used for the recruitment and development of employees in companies, the criteria used to make decisions were implicitly known to all parties involved. The approach taken by the decision makers, however, was not transparent nor objective nor democratic in accordance with equality of opportunity.

The recent changes resulting from West and East German cooperation, joint venture contracts, restructuring of East German companies, etc. suddenly created a need for methods to select suitable employees for certain (partly newly created) jobs as well as the need to assess the educational and promotional aspects of these applicants and to develop suitable training methods.

It was to be expected that every procedure which was different from previous ones would initially be readily accepted. The result was a flood of new methods and instruments which lacked, from our point of view, the following consideration: Is a country which was under a one-sided political influence for 40 years ready to take on a method such as, for example, the assessment centre (AC)? This procedure is based on the performance principle, which means each job applicant will do everything in his or her power to achieve the goal, i.e. to obtain the position. (In East Germany this had not previously been necessary, since everyone was automatically appointed to some post and had little chance of playing a part in the decision. On the other hand, no employee had to worry about losing his or her job.) The assessment centre is based on highly developed socializing between people. It can only achieve objective results if everyone follows certain rules and behaves in a fair, cooperative and 'democratic' manner. Experience of these behaviour patterns cannot be taken for granted for all groups in former East Germany.

When developing an AC for a different social group, surely the methodical principles of this procedure will have to apply in order to achieve the hoped-for results. We cannot rely only on our previous experiences with an AC in Western companies, but have to be continuously aware of the particular target group during each development and implementation step and have to adapt our procedure accordingly. We will list these steps below.

Later we will introduce for each step some experiences that we have gained. These experiences refer to the implementation of ACs for five different companies. The ACs were held either to select employees for companies starting up in former East Germany or were held for East German applicants who were to be appointed for the first time to a West German job. The number of ACs held by us varied according to the company, between three and 50. Our experience is based on rather unsystematic selective observation as well as on the systematic evaluation of available data.

The following steps are to be taken during the development and implementation of an AC:

- field analysis
- development of observation criteria and exercises
- training and instructing observers
- implementation of the AC
- discussing the results and the decision making
- feedback to the participants
- further development and promotion of the participants.

Field analysis   The analysis of environment is the first and most important part of an AC development, since its results will influence all subsequent steps. Here information is gathered from people who can describe the target positions and their requirements and to whom the working situation of future job holders is familiar. Observation criteria and exercises for the future AC should be developed according to the contents of these interviews.

The interviews will also help people to reflect on and structure their understanding and expectations (which are partly only subconscious) and to recognize deficiencies or unanswered queries, e.g. regarding the future tasks of the job holder.

For the development of an AC for former East Germany it is particularly important to include information on the group of people who will be applying. This information relates to professional and academic development, professional know-how, the existing technical standard at the previous job and also to the kind of cooperation, communication and leadership to which the potential applicant was previously accustomed. With this knowledge, exercises can be developed in accordance with the know-how and experience. The exercises will not only ensure that neither too much nor too little will be asked of the applicant, but will also offer a challenge to collaborate.

When planning the use of flipcharts for solving a given task (e.g. a group discussion) this would be quite a natural demand to Western applicants. Eastern applicants, on the other hand, very seldom make use of these visual aids.

The knowledge of the present situation and previous development of the future participant is just as important as information on future tasks and demands. Clients more often than not want a speedy completion of the ACs and initially do not appreciate the high degree of importance of the field analysis.

Development of observation criteria and exercises

The development of criteria and exercises is a process of continuous exchange between the client and the consulting institute. To achieve this, it is useful to establish a working group consisting of members of the employing company and the consulting institute. It is of the utmost importance that the working group also consists of people who are familiar with the situation in this culture, i.e. fellow countrymen of the prospective applicants.

Interviews for the field analysis with those who have knowledge of the future job situations also assists the development of criteria: this uncovers the abilities that future job holders should have in order to fulfil the demands of the role. For leaders of the team this could, for example, be leadership quality, flexibility, communication, initiative, etc. Participants in ACs will then be observed and assessed by these criteria.

Apart from the demands on the criteria that always apply, such as comprehensibility, independence and completeness, clear descriptions of criteria for all future users—from East and West—are required. This is necessary since the understanding of many terms differs owing to the different history of the two parts of the country. To give one example, the understanding of 'right' leadership behaviour in East Germany is probably different from that in West Germany. Certain behaviours may therefore be evaluated differently—positively and negatively—in the criterion 'leadership behaviour'.

For the working group this means that each criterion for assessment has to be defined clearly with concrete behaviour examples given, e.g. positive leadership behaviour means that someone delegates tasks, expresses appreciation as well as criticism, motivates the employees' interest for certain tasks, etc.

When developing suitable exercises for the AC, obviously the same principles apply as for the development of an AC in one's own social environment: the exercises should reflect the participant's future work situation, offer variety and should appeal to participants. They should ideally be equally difficult for all—no-one should have an advantage or disadvantage because of his or her specific professional knowledge. The tasks should also be capable of being solved, bearing in mind the previous knowledge and experience of the participants, if known—for instance, a group discussion on the topic of 'product promotion' would surely not have been feasible for applicants shortly after re-unification, since marketing was an unknown field in former East Germany until then. This has most probably changed now.

In addition, the phrasing of each exercise must always be checked by fellow countrymen for its comprehensibility by participants; for instance, anglicisms that we use in our speech daily, such as 'checklist' or 'know-how', may not be familiar to every participant. Another example is that means of visualization such as flipcharts, pinboards, etc. are seldom or only cautiously used during exercises—therefore their use has to be pointed out to the participants in a special way. On the other hand, applicants from East Germany, to take one example, seldom have to be reminded to put back material or use it economically since they usually do this of their own accord.

It is of the utmost importance to evaluate the experiences gained during each implementation and to make adjustments accordingly. These adjustments are particularly important in a society where information channels dating from pre-unification mean that the exercises of this new method become public knowledge quickly. This can distort the decisions on individuals' careers.

Training and instructing observers

Training and instructing observers in their responsibilities and tasks prepares them for their future activity. First, it must be decided of whom the group will consist. There are three possibilities:

1 observers from the West only
2 observers from the East only
3 mixed observer groups.

In the first group it might be assumed that the training and preparation of observers will be routine, since they have usually had experience with Western ACs. With regard to the target group, the standards often vary, however, and the assessment might be influenced by various motives (from leniency to lack of understanding); the extent and differentiation of the participant's knowledge will also vary. Furthermore, the observers' motivation will not be high when they are commissioned to the client's location as this often means less comfort in their accommodation and surroundings. This will thus automatically lead to fluctuations within the group of observers, and the possibility of gathering and utilizing experience of the new target group cannot be obtained.

If the group consists of East-observers only (East-observers refers to observers/assessors from former East Germany; West-observers to those from former West Germany—likewise with East-applicants, East-participants, etc.) then the motivation to play an active part in the procedure is generally quite high and therefore also the identification with the procedure. West-observers have difficulty in estimating the acceptance of observers by participants. For instance, acceptance can be quite low (almost non-existent), if the observer used to have certain high-level and influential political functions before the 'change'. Such individuals would often have had to deal with and assess people in their function and are most certainly good observers because of these experiences. However, their political background is reason enough that they are scarcely accepted as being 'objective observers', and they can thus harm the reputation of the procedure as normally being objective.

A study in which opinions on ACs from West German observers are compared with those of East German observers revealed the following results. Both observer groups were often involved in ACs. They were interviewed on their experiences gained as observer and their detailed opinion of the activity as assessor.

The West-observers often think of themselves as competent 'experts in methods', who give suggestions and propose further developments of the AC procedure. They feel they are the 'methodical conscience', responsible for following methodical rules, and they clearly emphasized this responsibility during the interviews. For some of them their own personal experience during their first involvement was most important.

The procedure is experienced by East-observers with curiosity, astonishment, 'stage fright' and a sense of fun. Questions regarding their personal responsibility towards the procedure and the participants form part of the personal analysis of the procedure. This perspective is mentioned more often by the experienced East-observers: they are confronted with a totally new procedure of personnel selection in which they come to conclusions by means of a democratic decision process. The different and unknown process and the unfamiliar task cause curiosity among the

East-observers, i.e. they wonder whether they will cope with this very new activity and are astonished when they realize that they have indeed managed to do the new job. The responsibility which each observer has towards self or others is also discussed frequently. The observation and the responsibility towards the participants are seen as a constant challenge.

Experienced West-observers furthermore discuss the significance of an AC to them in relation to their own learning. Assessment centres give them an intensive experience when assessing employees for a practical field. The combination of preliminary training measures, observer training, and 'testing it out' afterwards in a real situation which assists a company in recruiting suitable employees, is considered useful. The East-observers, on the other hand, hardly ever look at the AC procedure in this way. The reason for this could be that the former East German provinces do not yet have extensive learning programmes for management development and advancement. This means that structures will first have to be established.

From the perspective of company orientation, West-observers consider the procedure for its cost-effectiveness. The financial and personnel expenditure can be justified according to the effectiveness of the procedure to select future (junior) managers who fit into the company. Experienced East-observers describe the ACs more often under the company-orientated aspect. Because of the change in their professional activity, for instance, in a joint venture project and owing to confrontation with other 'Western' company structures and philosophies they are looking at new values such as teamwork. A question clearly arises for the East-observers in adopting these new values: is the AC procedure suitable to select future employees (for their own company) who can fulfil the 'new' requirements?

The third possibility is the mixed observer group. Already during the training period this arrangement has shown a high risk of East-observers feeling inferior towards the 'experienced' West-observers. Good supervision of the team could probably decrease this phenomenon. More obvious are the problems arising from the observers' different understanding of the language. We quote below a few observations made during evaluation meetings of ACs:

1 In the West *initiative* mostly stands for independent activity and would be described in an AC with the following behaviour pattern: 'Makes suggestions of own accord', 'Takes decisions independently' or 'Represents own point of view firmly to others'. For observers from ex-East Germany someone already shows initiative if carrying out a task by merely doing what he or she has been told (for instance by a manager). According to our understanding in the West this would stand for exactly the opposite, namely insufficient (independent) initiative.

2 A further discrepancy in the understanding of required characteristics shows in the criterion *'flexible thinking and acting'*. For
observers from the East this especially means the adaptation (which
certainly is very skilful) to prevailing conditions and may even mean
subordinating oneself, whereas for West-observers it would mean
to take up different, unusual and original points of view or
perspectives.

3 Similarly apparent is the difference in seeing the pattern of
communicating behaviour. During the evaluation in an AC in one of
the 'new' West German provinces, an observer from West Germany
described the communication pattern of an East-applicant as long-
winded, meaningless, not binding and uninformative to the
communication partner. His torrent of words contained mostly
empty wordshells, which also had no impact value. An East-observer,
on the other hand, described her impression of this applicant as
follows: 'The applicant was friendly towards his partner and gave
open as well as detailed information. He aroused interest and his
winning appearance brought about a positive working atmosphere.'
These different assessments of the behaviour of one person can, of
course, be attributed to various factors. From this example, however,
the listed difference can be put down to the different language
socialization of the two observers. The observer from the West
initially misunderstood the communicative behaviour shown since
the rules were unfamiliar to her. She could not have understood it
anyway, because the meaning of what someone does can only be
understood if the associated life-forms, language habits, observer and
assessment patterns are part of one's own life experience. Since this
was not the case the West-observer saw the behaviour of the
applicant in the eyes of her own linguistic background and described
her perception accordingly. The observer from the East, in contrast
to her colleague from the West, shared the common communication
background with the applicant; these internalized rules caused a
spontaneous and different understanding of the applicant's
behaviour. Admittedly, here the objection is, of course, that the
appearance of the applicant can only be judged as being suitable
under East German circumstances and would probably not satisfy the
requirements of the Western industrial world. The assessment of the
West-observer at least seems to say this. However, the above-
mentioned communication behaviour cannot be understood if it is
looked at only with regard to Western standards.

Implementation of the AC
Implementation of the AC begins with the briefing and introduction
given to the participants. Although this procedure is known to many
West-applicants (one can prepare oneself partly with the help of books)
it is completely new to East-applicants. For this reason transparency
and openness are even more important than would be the case for ACs
held in the West, and the establishing of confidence is a prerequisite for
the success of this procedure. It happens now and again that participants

who have applied cancel their application during the introduction and leave without giving a reason.

The implementation of an AC runs according to a strict timetable, to which all participants have to adhere. This timetable will show no formal differences no matter where the AC is held, the only difference being that East-participants are used to starting work much earlier in the morning (around 7 a.m.) and expect to leave work in the early afternoon (around 4 p.m.).

Discussing the results and the decision making

When looking at the discussion of results and the decision making, the question arises as to whether East-participants of ACs are assessed, on average, lower or higher than West-participants and, if so, in which criteria. Table 4.1 shows the results of seven ACs (= 84 participants) of East-applicants compared to results of seven ACs of West-applicants. These ACs were held during the period July 1990–May 1991 and were aimed to select trainees for a bank.

The results show that both applicant groups are effectively the same. They show only slightly lower ratings for East-applicants in all dimensions.

Looking at the observers' qualitative reports regarding the participants in each exercise, we get the following picture:

During the AC exercise 'simulation of a planning task' four participants solve a problem together. This exercise has various phases and in each phase new problems and information arise. Compared with other exercises observers here have the longest time to observe the participants. The verbal description by observers of the East-applicants' behaviour during this exercise tells us that the East-applicants are more reserved and less independent in their goal orientation. The same impression is

Table 4.1   *Average ratings in all exercises for all participants on eight criteria*

	East	West	Difference
Total average	4.46	4.57	−.11
Structured thinking and acting	4.45	4.60	−.15
Mental flexibility	4.46	4.58	−.12
Initiative and independence	4.54	4.70	−.16
Cooperation	4.48	4.50	−.02
Self-control	4.31	4.35	−.04
Perseverance and stress tolerance	4.63	4.72	−.09
Communication and social behaviour	4.32	4.44	−.12
Professional motivation	4.79	4.84	−.05

also gained in the AC exercise on negotiation. The East-applicant does not argue as assertively with partners when solving a problem. In general they do not follow their ideas as emphatically as West-applicants.

There are a few observers who took part in various ACs for East-applicants since July 1990. Their (verbally expressed) impression is that during this time East-applicants grew quickly closer to West-applicants, in their appearance, their self-confidence and the clarity of their professional goals.

This adaptation to 'Western' requirements will take place at different speeds, depending on the mental and physical closeness of the applicant to Western standards and companies. Maybe the adaptation is often only an outward one, whereas the actual views and ideas are not expressed.

Feedback to the participants

The feedback of results to participants is essential in all ACs. Each participant who undergoes this procedure has a right to be told how he or she was viewed by the observers. The feedback should whenever possible be given during a personal conversation.

The participant is given hints and recommendations for a further career, especially when being turned down in an AC. This step is extremely important for East-applicants, since they previously seldom had to attend examinations and assessments like these and experience a rejection as extremely depressing.

Further development and promotion of the participants

Participants who will receive an offer for the targeted position as a result of the AC should be helped by means of matching development measures according to their potential in the various fields. These developments are especially important to East-applicants in order to support them during their training in the new fields, technologies and unfamiliar working methods. This support is even more significant if the company's philosophy is far removed from that of former East German companies, and the identification of new goals is emphasized.

The more each employee is convinced that these new ideologies correspond to the human goals and ethical standards of cooperation, the sooner the change will take place.

Implications for cross-cultural assessment and development

1 Close attention needs to be given to the cultural history, conventions in work behaviour and the kind of communication used in cultural group(s) from which applicants and employees are drawn.
2 Although business practice between cultures often tends to 'converge' in time, different circumstances at any time, such as a different stage of privatization or development of a quality orientation, may cause extra difficulties of transfer of methods between one country and another.

3 The task force that is guiding the implementation of assessment and development initiatives should include people familiar with the culture(s) that are to be involved.
4 Performance criteria should be expressed in language that conveys the same understanding in all cultures represented, with behavioural examples, after full consultation with people who know all the cultures.
5 The content and wording of exercises should be checked by people from all cultures taking part. Unequal advantage should be identified and eliminated.
6 Assessors should be trained and 'managed' so that if a mix of cultures is involved all should feel on an equal footing.
7 Feedback and development need to be handled in a way which is sensitive to the customs and expectations of all groups.

References and further reading

Bolton, G.M. (1986) *Defining Managers' Jobs and Careers*, Roffey Park Institute, Horsham.

Bruchon-Schweitzer, M. and Ferrieux, D. (1991) 'Une enquête sur le recrutement en France', *Revue Européenne de Psychologie Appliquée*, 9–12.

European Survey on the Assessment Centre Method, paper presented at the 4th European Convention on Assessment Centre Methods, Venice, 15/16 October 1992.

Hill, R. (1994) *EuroManagers & Martians*, Europublications, Brussels.

Hofstede, G. (1984) *Culture's Consequences: international differences in work-related values*, Sage, London.

Hofstede, G. (1991) *Cultures and Organizations: software of the mind*, McGraw-Hill, Maidenhead.

McClelland, D.C. (1961) *The Achieving Society*, Van Nostrand, Princeton, N.J.

Shackleton, V. and Newell, S. (1991) 'Management selection: a comparative survey of methods used in top British and French companies', *Journal of Occupational Psychology*, 64, 23–36.

Shackleton, V. and Newell, S. (1993) 'How companies in Europe select their managers', *Selection and Development Review*, Vol. 9, No. 6.

Smith, P.B. (1992) 'Organizational behaviour and national cultures', *British Journal of Management*, Vol. 3, 39–51.

5 Assessment for development

Hélio Moreira and Lou Van Beirendonck

In this chapter we put the emphasis more fully on development, but show how this arises from defining the needs through the assessment process and from obtaining commitment to development from those who have participated in assessment. This is illustrated through a case based in Portugal but drawing on wider inputs and influences.

In the second part of the chapter Lou Van Beirendonck draws on his experience in Belgium to raise the important, but often neglected, question of whether or not development of some behavioural characteristics is possible. Motivation is certainly vital, but even then there may be limitations to 'trainability'.

A case for assessment and development

Background

The following case study is the result of work with a large national company in Portugal and took place during 1991 and 1992. The company had a monopoly in its field of activity and was characterized by a highly technological and product-based culture. Membership of the European Union, in conjunction with a policy of privatizations and indisputable signs given by the government that the company could well have to operate under competitive conditions, led the board of directors to initiate an accelerated process to transform company culture into one in which the customer came first and where service would assume precedence over technology and the product.

During the course of the work the government put the restructuring of the sector into effect, opening up some of the segments and markets which had previously been the exclusive domain of this company to private operators as well as deciding to merge and privatize the various companies which it owned in this sector.

Putting these policies into practice involved changes at a senior management level, and the project which commenced in 1991 with one board of directors was adapted to new requirements due to the employment of new directors. It was taken to the stage at which all the staff who had been initially planned for were incorporated.

Objectives   When the company asked for consultant help from ADQ at Egor Portugal the only thing we were sure of was that the company intended to alter its *modus operandi* so as to prepare for the future: it wished to change from a culture which valued consensus and avoided risks and confrontation to one where the managers show more confidence and initiative, where all the workers feel responsible for achieving objectives and are rewarded when this occurs and where the customer comes first.

Steps had been taken by the company previously to achieve this transformation: the first had been the reorganization of the company, which led to a reduction in the number of hierarchical levels in the structure, new divisions in the markets and a redefinition of the role of central services. There was also an increase in the responsibilities of the managers who were directly linked to each geographical market.

This process of change brought with it alterations in the various functional areas of the company as in many cases central responsibilities had been transferred to local levels. Nevertheless, the central management bodies were to continue in a supportive and coordinating role, setting objectives and monitoring the same as well as approving resources and means.

The commercial management function was one of those which endeavoured to prepare itself for this transformation, concerning itself with the selection and training of the permanent staff who were to be responsible at a local level for the sales of company products and services and consequently to whom many of the activities performed at present by the central commercial management were to be transferred.

The member of the board of directors in charge of the commercial sector decided to put this process of change in corporate culture into motion by selecting and training those to be responsible for the commercial function in each geographical area, i.e. commercial managers. In hierarchical terms they were responsible to the general manager of their geographical area and had under their control the team of sales and after-sales staff for the various products and services which were available there. In functional terms they were responsible to product managers and the marketing department in Lisbon.

The company's Head of Human Resources decided to create a task force presided over by the training manager and comprising those who were responsible for assessment and training, as well as ADQ as external consultant. Other members were introduced into this group, in particular commercial and marketing management staff, in accordance with the problems which existed and the decisions being taken. The group's responsibilities included agreeing with the customer (the board member for the commercial sector) the objectives to be accomplished by the project, its planning, the organization of resources, the implementation of measures and/or monitoring of the latter.

The main objectives to be accomplished were as follows:

- to assess a group of candidates for the new job of commercial manager for each of the various geographical areas
- to train those selected, paying special attention to the strengths and weaknesses which became apparent during the course of the assessment procedure.

However, for the project to be considered a success it needed to respect the following specifications:

1 It should take a maximum period of three months.
2 It should take into account the new responsibilities and skills required for the post.
3 It should keep those people who were to be included in the process involved and productive rather than apprehensive and under-confident in their ability to perform their new functions.
4 The customer should be kept sufficiently informed to be enabled to decide which option would be best whenever there were any doubts about what would be required.
5 The cooperation of the people from the various geographical areas and from the other human resources departments should be retained.
6 There must be the flexibility to incorporate different ideas and unexpected alterations resulting from the transformations which the company was undergoing.

Assess to develop   To accomplish the aforementioned objectives it was decided to divide up the work and carry it out in various stages, the objectives, participants and methods of which are summarized in Figure 5.1.

The group proposed and coordinated the establishment of a training plan comprising the whole operational managing structure of the commercial board at a national level. After being duly discussed with the top management group this plan was put into practice. Concerning the training programme itself, this involved the undertaking of actions divided into three groups: determination of the needs both of the company and each participant; the drawing up of the best solutions; and the establishment and assurance of the results individually. In practice, this was a process divided into five phases adapted to all functional levels, as follows:

1 *Identification of the responsibilities, skills and attitudes*   The purpose of this phase is to determine what is expected to be done and how. Having this in mind we appealed to multidisciplinary teams, including employees involved in the restructuring, other persons with experience of this type of situation, and clients, since this whole

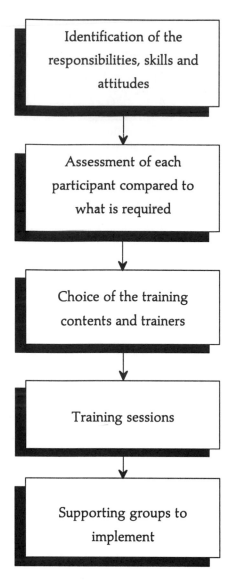

Figure 5.1   *The five phases of the project*

process aims to satisfy their needs. The final result is a list describing the new responsibilities and the appropriate attitudes.

2 *Assessment of each participant compared to what is required*   In this phase each participant is assessed and receives feedback regarding strong and weak points. The chosen method—assessment centres— puts each person in circumstances simulating reality and feedback is given according to the participant's performance. The aim is to identify strong and weak points in order to establish learning goals. Future senior managers and people from human resources functions were trained as observers. The first obstacle to overcome was to

convince the managers that assessment of potential staff members is not solely the domain of human resources people. Subsequently they considered that it was extremely useful for them to undergo this procedure for the following reasons:

- it elucidates the process itself
- owing to the greater knowledge which they gained of the assessment criteria. Most of them had not been involved in previous phases of the project
- they acquire the ability to supplement and understand better the information which they receive about their staff
- owing to the understanding and 'fine-tuning' of language which makes dialogue with their colleagues easier, including that relating to the training programme which the latter are experiencing.

During the observers' training course a minimum profile for the post was drawn up once each criterion had been discussed in detail.

The assessment was undertaken with a custom-designed programme, embracing a whole range of situations which tested the agreed criteria: these included 'customer' and 'fellow staff' situations, planning of measures, etc. Given the degree of responsibility and the complexity of the tasks which were to be allocated to the future commercial managers, the programme was relatively extensive and arduous, both for candidates and observers. It took one and a half days for the candidates and half a day for observers to produce conclusions on each candidate.

The evaluation meetings proved to be very lively, there being a great deal of material for discussion, and consequently also quite long. Practice has shown that the less experience the observers possess the greater the tendency to prolong meetings: there is more repetition of information and a greater tendency for each to defend his or her scores.

Based on the information gained from the meetings individual reports and profiles were drawn up which were made available to the managers and to the person assessed and served as the basis for appointments made by the company. Following this was the interview feedback stage: each candidate was informed in a personal interview of what had been said about him or her in the evaluation process. The interviews were held by those in charge of the project and they took place prior to the start of the training procedure. This meant that people would be aware of the areas which they needed to work on and more at ease about them by the time they started the training.

Candidates who had not been appointed to be commercial managers were also interviewed.

During this stage the following methodology was used:

- informing the candidate of the assessment criteria
- requesting him or her to carry out a self-assessment, giving him/

herself a score of from 1 to 5 in accordance with what he or she remembers having done at the assessment session, helping him or her to identify the exercise(s) which was suited to each criterion whenever this should prove necessary
- informing him or her of the observing group's observations both in quantitative and qualitative terms (final grade)
- assessment by the candidate of the assessment centre procedure.

On the whole the candidates produced self-assessment comments similar to those which had been produced by the observers. The majority of candidates assessed the procedure as being extremely useful in terms of self-discovery and they believed that having access to this information prior to training would enable them to make more of the training. There was a generally good response to the opportunity to find out what the company required of them in behavioural terms.

3 *Choice of the training contents and trainers*   The choice of the contents reflects the competences and attitudes that are to be developed. At the end of the session each participant should be able to identify clearly what he or she is expected to do, how he or she is going to be assessed and to have tried successfully the new behaviours and attitudes. This choice was carried out by a multidisciplinary team formed by experts external and internal to the company who included consultants from different countries (mainly Roffey Park Institute in Britain) and proved to be very positive, allowing a cross-fertilization of experiences. The preparatory meetings often stimulated the creation of new working tools or procedures.

4 *Training sessions*   The training sessions were designed in a way which allowed plenty of experimentation and feedback from the trainer. Real case studies based on the company materials were designed in order that the candidates could work and get acquainted with their future working tools. The format of the course included groups of 12 participants during two-and-a-half weeks' residential training covering three different areas:

- the company's products, services, strategy and future organization
- management and self-development themes
- selling, marketing and distribution of services and products.

5 *Supporting groups to implement*   At the end of classroom training each participant had to make a plan for his or her return to work which was the basis for the implementation groups. These groups were established by participants according to geographical affinities, and met one afternoon every month. Their objective was to help each participant to implement individual plans, using the other participants and an external consultant as mentors.

The feedback of participants and managers was very impressive, and at the end of the project conducted for the commercial managers described above the company requested the task force to deal with the training of product managers from the central marketing structure, heads of sales and salespeople for their specific geographical areas. This was undertaken by late 1992 and early 1993.

Considerations and major conclusions

A new board of directors appointed by the government took office at the end of 1992. A new organizational structure was approved for the company, but with the subsequent alteration in the commercial organization for the specific geographical areas, in responsibilities and in people, a follow-up procedure was difficult to implement. However, some considerations are worth recording.

First, the project was completed within the deadline and in accordance with the specifications, and the task force was given new orders.

Second, all those taking part, be they managers, human resources technical staff, candidates or trainees, emphasize the importance of the project for the rapid implementation of the new structure and the creation of a new style of reporting between the central human resources department and the geographical business areas. The former began to interrelate more with those responsible for operations, supporting the geographical business areas and sometimes acting as their consultant, even in areas which were outside the scope of the project. This is best demonstrated by the fact that some of the human resources staff left that function and are now working alongside the operational managers with whom they had worked most closely during the course of the project.

Third, candidates assessed and trained believe that this project had personal consequences which enabled them to gain greater maturity and more professional security. However, they regret that in many circumstances the 'whirl' of transformations which the company has undergone or which it is undergoing has not enabled all of them to realize the ideas and plans which they intended to put into practice.

Finally, the company became better known because the Portuguese trade press published what had been done, interviewing those who had taken part in the project and describing the method followed.

Practical implications

Participation in this project has led us to various conclusions, and we would like to draw attention to them for those readers who are confronted with similar situations:

1 It is vital that a task force be created for the design and implementation of the project; however, let us not forget to integrate into the company's usual practices the knowledge gained during the course of the project, namely in terms of staff training, assessment policies and practices as well as consultation with the operational managers. Otherwise we run the risk of going back to square one after completing the project, the company losing not only the know-how gained but also the commitment and involvement of human

resources staff, as they will find it difficult to return to doing things in the old way.

2 Clarify with senior management how long the organizational transformations are to be in force so that the assessment and training programmes can be designed bearing in mind what is going to happen; and also within what time period and in what way it is hoped to obtain the results of the investment which has been made. This is intended to make it possible to know whether or not people will have sufficient time to put what they have learned into practice before moving on to new responsibilities resulting from a new reorganization. In addition, try to ascertain whether the type of results expected may be obtained or not within the said time period and if it is possible to achieve them merely by resorting to training.

3 Make sure that the whole company has been informed of the project so as to reach and involve all those who are upstream and downstream of the function for which the new people have been trained (for example, by means of an internal newsletter).

4 It is essential to prepare the hierarchical and functional structure—which the trainees will later have to deal with—for the changes in attitude and skills. This is necessary because the work systems and habits which were around were intended for the very reality which it had been intended to change. The company is obviously not going to invest in training if it is then going to ask employees to do the same thing as before and rely on them in exactly the same way as before, or even reproach them for displaying new attitudes and endeavouring to take part in areas where they believe they have added skills. For this purpose we believe it is vital that small seminars are held to explain what is going to be done and how and what it is hoped the *modus operandi* will be for those who have the closest contact with these trainees.

Trainability of skills

Assessment centres and development

At nearly all assessment centres which we have seen over the past 10 years, we have had intensive, constructive and mostly lengthy talks with the assessors after the simulations about the future of the assessees. What were the observations during the assessment centre and what do they imply for the further career of the respective assessees? This is a vital question. Whether this is an assessment within the framework of selection, promotion or possibilities for development, or a general screening of strengths and weaknesses, they all have one thing in common: we are interested in the future behaviours of colleagues or in the possibility that they may acquire a specific behavioural pattern.

In assessment with respect to promotion or selection we have established that on the whole about 70 per cent of the advice is of a 'yes, but ...' nature. Advice which is downright explicitly favourable seldom occurs (about 10 per cent), whereas almost 20 per cent of the advice is unfavourable with respect to development or promotion to another/higher position. This unfavourable advice is related to the fact that the assessees can present themselves much better for another direction/position than the one for which they are being assessed, or because they have too far to go in their growth and development process to satisfy the desired profile for a specific position.

Thus in the majority of cases advice is conditional. In many cases advice boiling down to 'yes, subject to training of some kind' is formulated because the assessee lives up to the profile on the whole and because it is assumed that the shortcomings in his or her profile are trainable. Training is often the (apparent) life-saver.

The training manager is informed and receives a survey of the points for development, and the case is closed.

In the past this situation has more than once been the beginning of a long silence. The development of a training programme on 'Persuasiveness' is not easy to achieve and certainly not economic if it concerns one or two trainees only. Other themes such as 'individual leadership' already exist as part of a long-term training programme. The traditional training programmes are generally educational and are often not geared to the training of specific behavioural characteristics. This has resulted in little coaching or training being provided. We have to acknowledge that a number of assessees failed again in a 'second-chance assessment' because they were insufficiently trained or supported after the first assessment centre session.

Some questions on trainability

If we place the above phenomena in a period of economic growth and of scarceness of well-qualified personnel (end of the eighties), then it is understandable that assessment centre specialists have since then concerned themselves with the following questions: Are all behavioural criteria trainable? Are all people equally receptive to training? Which is the best way to train human behaviour?

More than once we have organized workshops, together with training managers, human resources managers and consultants, to consider the question whether behavioural criteria are trainable. Every time this resulted in a discussion about conviction, portrayals of man (humankind) and belief. We went home carrying a list of influencing factors on the trainability or otherwise of behaviour.

These factors may roughly be divided into two categories. First we discuss individual characteristics influencing the trainability of behaviour. Then we discuss the influence of environmental factors.

Finally, we illustrate for a number of behavioural criteria to what extent and in what manner they are trainable, independent of the individual and environmental factors.

Individual factors   There are various individual properties which have an important influence on the trainability of behaviour. Some of those properties are relatively stable and unchangeable in time, e.g. intellectual capacities, personality, etc. Others have a situational or temporary character and may therefore be influenced, e.g. motivation, expectations, standards.

Ability to learn   For the acquisition of behavioural skills it is important that specific cognitive capacities be sufficiently present. That is the reason, by the way, why we plead for the expansion of an assessment centre session with an investigation into the cognitive capacities, in which separate aspects of cognition are measured: divergent thinking, convergent thinking, abstract reasoning skill, etc.

If individuals possess a certain degree of cognitive capacities, this will not only influence the speed of their learning but will also determine to a considerable extent whether various behavioural characteristics are trainable. For example: 'Abstraction' and 'Judgement' respectively are an intellectual capacity and a behavioural dimension which are closely connected. The intellectual basis to a large extent determines the train-ability of behaviour.

Willingness to learn   In our view, the willingness to learn is a combination of different elements:

● *Fit with career expectations*   First there are career expectations. If someone is keenly interested in achieving a certain job level, and if it should appear that a specific shortcoming must be remedied to achieve it, that person will naturally be inclined much sooner to release more energy to learn extra things. The urge to achieve some-thing is a determining factor for the success of training efforts. In an assessment centre essentially an evaluation is made as to whether an assessee can do what is expected of him or her over a period of time. What the assessee really wants needs also to be part of a thorough examination, however, and this has important implications for the trainability as such.

It sometimes happens that an assessment centre session, despite preliminary talks with assessees, must be supplemented with a career discussion. The focus in such a discussion is on the assessee's short- and long-term expectations.

The success of training efforts is strongly influenced by the extent to which the behaviour to be trained is connected with the trainee's career expectations. When the behaviour to be trained fits insuffi-ciently into the career ambition, then there is a limited chance of success.

● *Openness to feedback*   Another success factor is the openness to feedback. Defensive reactions from the assessee to feedback on behaviour are indications for limited success of relevant training efforts. In the assessment centre for line operations at General Motors, Antwerp, the assessees get feedback during the performance of their tasks. In that way it can be estimated to what extent they are open to feedback and how quickly they can integrate information in the performance of their tasks. In addition, after the performance of their tasks they are asked what they would do differently in future. The openness to feedback may also be evaluated by using video-feedback. After the assessment centre session the candidate is given the opportunity to look at his or her own behaviour and to evaluate it. One of the assessors is present at this session and evaluates the assessee's verbal and non-verbal reactions. The extent to which the assessee is able to reflect openly and critically upon himself/herself is one of the indicators which helps to determine the trainability of behaviour that has weaknesses.

- *Preferred ways of learning* The willingness, but also the ability to learn, is influenced by the way in which learning instructions are presented. Some people still have an aversion to computers. According to the doctrine of Neuro-Linguistic-Programming (NLP), we all have a preferred channel through which we communicate and learn; for example, someone with a strongly auditory orientation will learn best through spoken language.

  Special attention must be devoted to the growing interest of training institutes in computer-aided training programmes.

Values and norms Values, norms and convictions are programmes which we use in our daily activities. They determine our conduct to a large extent. Examples are the portrayals of mankind which we use (Theory X: people are by nature lazy and must be activated by third persons, versus Theory Y: people are by nature driven to achieve delegated goals and are capable, to a high degree, of directing and activating themselves); the perception of the role of the manager; formation of images of others and oneself.

In a global assessment centre a screening of values and norms may form part of the assessment. If we are to know the true significance of the manifested behaviour, then we shall have to be able to judge the underlying values.

For the training and education of behavioural skills, too, an insight into the assessee's pattern of values is essential. Values, norms and convictions influence behaviour, but they can be influenced themselves as well.

Personality Developmental psychologists agree that our personality is shaped to a large extent and that there is very little, if anything, that we can change about it, especially in adults. Personality characteristics are also described as 'relatively stable dispositions'. Personality characteristics influence behaviour, but are not necessarily demonstrated in behaviour. Let us give an example of strain or stress: I may have a nervous disposition, but maybe I have learned to suppress this in such a way that other people cannot detect any nervousness. I may have learned to control familiar situations, and to anticipate the expected stress. In new, unexpected and stressful situations, however, there is a real chance of my falling back to my innermost individuality, my personality.

All the aforementioned factors influence the trainability of behaviour at the level of the individual. If we want to be able to judge the trainability of behaviour, then we shall have to know all the above elements.

We have visualized a model about the influence of these factors on behaviour and on its trainability, the 'Influencing Interaction and

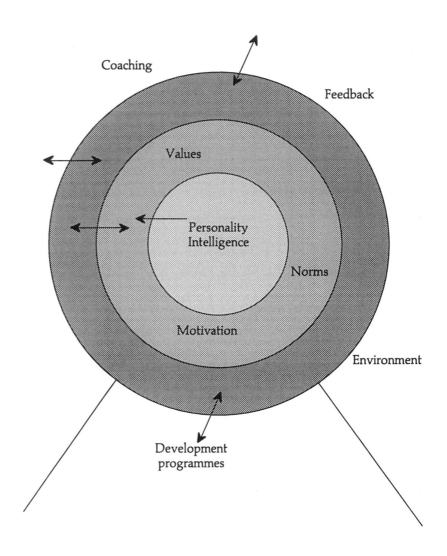

Modification Model', as shown in Figure 5.2.

Figure 5.2 *Influencing interaction and modification model*
Our behaviour is directed by personal, internal factors. Some of those factors cannot be influenced, or hardly at all, but they do influence our behaviour: personality, intelligence, etc. Other personal factors in themselves are the result of interaction between the individual and the environment; they are the result of learning processes, education and experience. They are the thought patterns, the values and convictions which significantly determine our behaviour. 'Motivation' may be regarded as a conviction which stimulates goal-directed behaviour. Apart from the internal, personal factors which influence our behaviour, there are also numerous environmental factors. The extent to which personal factors or environmental factors determine our behaviour may then be said to depend on the personal conviction 'I can or cannot influence my environment' or, in other words, on the extent of 'internal locus of control'.

How do we learn? Through learning we are better able to adapt to new or changing circumstances. We get new ideas, we cultivate habits and we develop behavioural skills. Through continuous learning we anticipate the future. By developing our skills we increase our chances of survival.

Since Pavlov published his Classical Conditioning Theory, a lot of systematic research has been conducted into the way in which we learn. Thorndike showed, through experimental investigation, that the consequences of our behaviour strongly influence learning behaviour (the Law of Effect). When we obtain a positive reaction to manifest behaviour, the relevant behaviour will consequently be reinforced. Skinner arrived at the conclusion that it is possible to change behaviour by changing its consequences (Antecedent Behaviour Consequences). These insights are fundamental for an understanding of people's learning behaviour.

Kolb and others showed that adults learn especially by gaining experience. Being confronted with tasks and assignments and getting the opportunity to learn 'by experience' also turns out to be preferred in trade and industry. 'Trial-and-error learning' accounts for almost 50 per cent of acquired behaviour—half of everything we learn in an enterprise we have acquired on-the-job. Thirty per cent of what we learn in a company is derived from personal coaching, discussions with managers, coaches and mentors. Only 20 per cent of what we learn is achieved by 'Education and Training' (Source: Honeywell Development Center Europe).

These conclusions have important consequences for the enterprise which wants to make the appropriate efforts to optimize the capacities, knowledge and skills of its employees. First, there is a tendency towards a more individual (tailor-made) approach. General educational programmes are substituted or supplemented by specific training and coaching efforts geared to the individual. In addition, there is a growing tendency towards the transfer of responsibility; the trainee is expected to help direct and regulate his or her personal training. These two tendencies are proved by the ever-increasing interest in individual coaching, mentoring and self-managed learning.

Environmental factors

Let us have another look at the Influencing Interaction and Modification Model. Environmental factors are of crucial importance to the training (conditioning) of behaviour. The daily receiving of feedback (verbally or behaviourally) from colleagues or managers and the gaining of experiences have a greater impact on our development than traditional development programmes. Informal feedback, experiences, coaching and mentoring are important influencing factors. The culture of the organization, the body of customs and usages, the examples in our immediate environment, unmistakably influence our own behaviour. Albert Schweitzer expressed his insight in this connection as follows: 'Example is not the main thing in influencing people, ... it's the only thing.'

Environmental factors influence our behaviour, but also play a role in determining values, norms and convictions, either directly or through behaviour. For example, if I as a manager am convinced that a directive approach is always to be preferred, discussions with colleagues, managers and trainers may induce me to understand that a participative approach may also lead to good results under specific circumstances; not only through discussion, but also under the influence of examples from others, it may be possible for me to adjust my basic ideas and principles. Those changed insights may be the basis of another, more participative behavioural approach. With reference to the IIM Model, it is the environmental factors that influence norms, insights and values, all of which in their turn initiate behavioural changes.

Another way of learning links up better with Thorndike's 'Law of Effect'. Referring to the same example of the directive manager, this may run as follows: in a training programme on leadership for example, I am asked as a directive manager in a simulation to approach a troublesome employee in a participative manner. In this simulation I experience that such an approach yields good results. Even though I may previously have been convinced that a good manager deals with employees in a directive manner, in the simulation I have found that a participative and less directive approach can be very successful. As a result of that behavioural experience I adjust my own ideas and principles, which may form the beginning of a behavioural change in this and similar situations.

Trainability of behavioural dimensions

Apart from the individual possibility for realizing individual behavioural changes, it is important to know which specific behavioural criteria are trainable 'in themselves'. We will for the time being stick to the hypothesis that some behavioural criteria are stable dispositions in the form of personality characteristics, and that they are consequently not trainable, or only to a limited extent.

Table 5.1 shows a survey of the trainability of behavioural characteristics. It also indicates in what ways they may be trained. The training possibilities indicated are examples (there are, of course, further possibilities). We then go on to discuss briefly those criteria which, in our view, are not trainable.

The findings in this survey are the result of the integration of know-how from assessment centres on the one hand with behavioural training on the other hand. Our findings have been thoroughly discussed with various colleagues in the field.

Non-trainable behavioural criteria Not all behavioural criteria are trainable. Some behavioural characteristics are strongly determined by personal attributes that cannot be influenced, such as intelligence and personality. We shall elucidate why these behavioural characteristics are scarcely trainable or not trainable.

Sociability Being able to adapt oneself in various social situations depends to a large extent on the basic personality of the individual. A person can may be trained to be 'sociable', e.g. at a trade fair, but it is difficult to generalize this acquired behaviour for other social situations, such as, for example, a wedding reception where you do not know anyone.

Need for achievement This is difficult to train as a relatively stable dimension. One can be situationally stimulated to achieve, either by commitment to the job, or by external reinforcers. Then the need for achievement subsequently depends on these environmental factors, and once they are gone the need for achievement will weaken as well.

Enthusiasm The same reasoning may be followed as for need for achievement.

Ability to learn A person can be trained in a system or in techniques to facilitate his or her learning, but the trainability as such is strongly limited by the available intellectual abilities.

Formation of judgement The faculty to assess a situation and to make a judgement on a quantity of data may be situationally trained. However, the acquired faculty of judgement in one situation is difficult to transfer to another situation. One may be taught, for instance, to apply insights into company strategy to a specific company situation, but in a new situation or in a different context, politics for instance, the faculty of making judgements will have been influenced to a limited extent only by the training efforts in the other context.

Vision The same reasoning may be followed as for formation of judgement. Moreover, the capacity to assess long-term effects or to oversee complex situations (helicopter view) depends on the ability for abstract and convergent reasoning (intelligence).

Table 5.1 *Trainability of behavioural characteristics*

	Not/Hardly trainable	Job assignment and experience	Coaching and mentorship	Education and training	Sample behaviour
Communicative skills					
Oral communication		Create opportunities to speak in group, make responsible for informing others.	Give feedback. 'Say it in your words?' 'What do you want to say?' 'Say it shorter.'	Communication training, training in presentation skills, audio and video feedback.	Show example behaviour and explain why and/or how.
Listening		Give the role of recorder or facilitator in a meeting, ask to report.	Listening tests, process stops in a dialogue.	Communication training, focusing on receptive behaviour.	Show example behaviour and explain why and/or how.
Impact (influence)		Give project responsibility, ask to defend a point of view.	Coaching in preparing on a strategy and on the arguments for a debate.	Communication training (non-verbal behaviour, NLP techniques, etc.)	Show example behaviour and explain why and/or how.
Management					
Delegation		Give a lot of work to do, set time limits, mention 'delegation'.	Confront on resistances, discuss actual tasks (who could also do this?).	Read a book (influences knowledge and ideas), training in coaching techniques.	Show example behaviour and explain why and/or how.
Planning and Organizing		Give responsibilities and set time limits, ask for weekly planning.	Discuss badly planned projects and look for opportunities to solve.	Train in time management techniques. Work with in-tray or other planning and organizing simulations.	Show example behaviour, be intolerant for a 'we will see' mentality.
Administrative skills		Work together with a good administrator, ask for feedback on systems.	Question goals, give feedback on daily work, discuss opportunities.	Secretary training, gather information on filing systems, PC training.	Show example behaviour and explain why and/or how.
Vision	X				
Leadership					
Group-oriented leadership		Create opportunities: project leadership, chairman of a meeting, etc.	Discuss situations of lack of/too much control or guidance.	Traditional leadership training, outdoor training, reading books (ideas).	Show example behaviour and explain why and/or how.

	Not/Hardly trainable	Job assignment and experience	Coaching and mentorship	Education and training	Sample behaviour
Problem-solving behaviour					
Problem analysis		Work together on a project with an 'analyst', work on complex problems.	Discuss complex problems, ask for information (How about ...), give feedback on the process.	Learn problem analysis solving techniques.	Show example behaviour and explain why and/or how.
Judgement	X				
Initiative		Project responsibility: chairman of a meeting, 'carte blanche' atmosphere.	Help in transferring ideas into proposals/ actions, give 'why-not' feedback.	Limited training possible in internal locus of control, NLP techniques.	Show example behaviour, programme on the desired atmosphere.
Decisiveness		Set time limits for decisions, give responsibility and offer support instead of taking responsibility and asking for support.	'A decision is not the same as a conclusion', give feedback and support the process (problem analysis, judgement, decision taking), support in dealing with uncertainties.	Read books of 'decision makers' (insight). Training in decision models.	Show example behaviour and explain why and/or how.
Social behaviour					
Team spirit		Involve in group or departmental projects with a high interdependency.	Discuss and redefine experiences in working together, feedback on behaviour.	Outdoor group training, consensus exercises, show profit of teamwork.	Show example behaviour, appreciation of group performances (bonus, etc).
Empathy			Focus on other people's point of view, 'feelings are facts'.	Train in 'gaining awareness' and in communication techniques in delicate situations.	Show example behaviour and explain why and/or how.
Sociability	X				
Motivational behaviour					
Motivation to achieve	X				
Enthusiasm	X				
Personal development					
Self-insight		An experience can give better self-insight, but usually it has to be combined with feedback.	Raise questions on performance and relations, give feedback.	Self-insight assessment centres.	Evaluate own performances and create an open, non-defensive atmosphere.
Learning ability	X				

Conclusion   We have described ways in which behaviour may be trained and the factors playing a role in that process. We have also described which behavioural dimensions are trainable and which ones cannot be influenced, or only to a limited extent. These insights have been established on the basis of our own training experience and also by exchanging experiences with various Belgian training managers.

From an international perspective it would be useful to test these findings and experiences systematically against those of trainers from other countries. Apart from possible intercultural differences in connection with the trainability of behaviour, we all function according to a number of similar basic mechanisms and answer to common qualities (we are all different but all the same). In this respect we expect that most of the Belgian findings described may also apply to and be used by others.

What is true in many things goes for the trainability of behaviour, too: 'Not everything, but a great deal, depends on the individuals themselves'. The willingness to change and the conviction that training efforts will yield results are essential determinants for success.

References and   Broad, M.L. and Newstorm, J.W. (1992) *Transfer of Training*, Addison Wesley,
further reading   Massachusetts.
Davis, B.L. (1992) *Successful Manager's Handbook: development suggestions for
         today's managers*, Personnel Decisions, New York.

6 Emerging issues in assessment and development

Robert Bols, Jos van Bree, Mac Bolton and Jan Gijswijt

In this chapter we look at a number of developments taking place in assessment methods and issues that are likely to affect attempts to use sophisticated tools like the assessment centre, taking account of the pressures and changes in international business life being experienced in the nineties. We also look at the way in which assumptions about employee development have been changing, with the ownership and responsibility for development shifting from the employer more towards the individual.

As the contributors to this book were brought together initially by a common interest in the assessment centre method forming Assessment Circle Europe, we first look at the state of this method and whether it has a future. Then we consider a few of the developments in the method that are becoming available and finally we face up to some of the difficulties in applying this and other methods in flatter hierarchies and in the international field of operations in which companies need to operate.

What is the state of the assessment centre method?

We need first to set the assessment centre method (ACM) in some kind of context. The origins provide us with one kind of context in which the emphasis was primarily on prediction of performance in a role not yet occupied, and other concerns of human resource management, such as training needs and defining development plans, were secondary. In part this was caused by an interest in establishing the predictive validity of the method (for example, Huck, 1973), and in such cases any resulting training and development interventions would contaminate the results. Thus ACM was seen as a method of assessing patterns of human behaviour by applying a systematic assessment methodology to representative situations or role-playing, relevant to the post or career in question. The situational exercises or role-plays are derived from a job analysis that highlights the critical situations encountered in the job or career. The behaviour sought during the critical situations is described in detail in the job analysis. This, in turn, is translated into *behaviour categories* or *behaviour criteria*. This methodology used the important principle that a person's overall assessment (from exercises, role-playing and relating them to the behaviour criteria) is based on the collective observations of several assessors.

Variations

Within the perspective outlined above there exists, however, room enough to apply the method in different ways. These different ways actually exist by virtue of the fact that we can no longer talk of a kind of 'standard assessment centre'. Each centre is different, not only in terms of the methods applied (role-playing, written exercises, discussion groups, personality questionnaires, intelligence tests, behaviour-oriented interviews, in-depth interviews, etc.), but also in terms of execution (context factors, including the way in which the role-players take part in defining the context). In the main, these variations arise from the centre's aim, which could be selection or promotion or identification of training needs or for development or career guidance. There may be variations also arising from the particular target group (e.g. internal or external participants) and the criteria used, not to mention the special points stressed by individual assessment users.

In addition, we could include a number of variations in the way the ACM is applied because of changes in the business scene, for instance limiting the number of assessors available in one place at a time or enabling participants to be assessed more individually rather than needing a significant number to be brought together at once. Some of these issues will be picked up later in this chapter.

ACM as an integrator of human resource management

It is becoming increasingly possible to see ACM not as an isolated tool but as a means of linking various parts of human resource management. If the job analysis and behaviour criteria have been soundly and thoroughly established, the observation of the required behaviour can be taken beyond selection role-playing to enable reliable assessment methodology to be used at other stages. By viewing the ACM in this way it becomes clear that the method is potentially more than an isolated tool, but represents a basic methodology from which to build an *integrated* HRM tool-kit. Thus the ACM acts more like a computer operating system than a specific application. The Michigan Model (Fombrun, Tichy and Devanna, 1984) gives the pillars of the human resource management cycle as selection (including promotion and placement), appraisal, rewards and development (see Figure 6.1). The assessment methodology is active in all these aspects, not least by providing a constant throughout the cycle.

Following selection/promotion the employee's profile on the criteria can be used to plan the induction and initial performance expected of him or her. The ideal profile expressed in behaviour criteria can be clearly described and the employee therefore learns a broad outline of

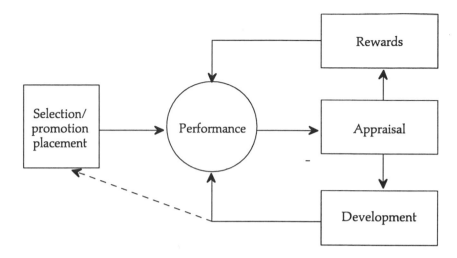

Figure 6.1 *The Michigan Model: The Human Resource Cycle* (reproduced by permission of John Wiley & Sons Inc., from *Strategic Human Resource Management*, Fombrun *et al.*, 1984)

how he or she is to perform and can look to his or her manager for advice. This would be much more difficult if the ideal profile were described merely in vague concepts such as maturity.

The next stage, that of appraisal, would involve assessing the employee against the same profile. Criteria-orientated appraisal has much in common with criteria-oriented selection as the same behaviour is being assessed. The only difference is that in appraisal the information is being gathered by observations spread over a longer time. It is an impossible task for the manager to carry out a permanent assessment of all staff in all of their activities and actions (especially as their numbers tend to grow the more the organization flattens). In other words, the manager must be selective. To keep this selectivity on a fair and even keel, and to ensure that it is not directed solely by random events, the manager should really concentrate on situations akin to the critical situations that surfaced during the job analysis. Training as an assessor as part of ACM greatly assists this process. Rewards, determined by job evaluation or performance-related pay, would benefit similarly from ACM as well as from more normal determinants.

Development of the employee

One of the ways in which ACM has been extended while keeping its essential methodology is in using assessments as a stimulus for all kinds of development of the participants. This extension is available even if the primary aim is selection/promotion. The collection of reliable information on strengths and weaknesses is a valuable opportunity which can, with the small extra effort needed, be turned into material to stimulate development. This has become more important in current conditions where opportunities for promotion are less numerous and many people who perform their jobs well need to be encouraged to see the future in terms of development without obvious promotion.

Examples are given in other chapters of the increased attention being given to the support of employee development. In some countries there has been a trend towards using the term 'development centre', in place of 'assessment centre'. Often the change of emphasis has not actually been very great, but there has been a gain in reduced anxiety—participants find the term 'development' more friendly and less threatening than 'assessment'. If the aim is genuinely directed towards the development of all participants then the development centre title is justified and honest. If, however, there are mixed aims, and some sponsoring managers are using the activity to select people (positively and/or negatively), the title will be seen as the sham it actually is, and the motivation to see it as an open opportunity for development will suffer.

Can we change the assessment centre method?

We have argued above that some changes have taken place and need to be made in order to match the various objectives. The ACM has long been the method of pragmatists. It was not developed from theoretical models, but from practice, from the idea that if you want to know whether someone can do something well you should assess him or her in situations where the skills have an opportunity to be shown. Even the behaviour criteria used in ACM are drawn up in the language of management rather than in that of psychology. Nevertheless, even with a pragmatic point of departure the ACM has always had to prove itself and enforce itself. This is evident from the mere fact that the vast majority of theoretical studies dealing with the method, certainly in the early years, are validation studies, or, in other words, studies designed to prove that the method actually measures what it claims to measure.

There would be no sense in sticking to an established pattern if it became clear that the time demands on observers, role-players and assessors had become unacceptable in current business conditions. Experiments and modifications will be essential if this work is to continue, although regular checks on validity are highly desirable. There could, of course, come a point where the fundamental principles were lost, and at one extreme an assessment centre could become no different from a development programme and at the other extreme it would be limited to interviews and individual paper-and-pencil tests, which offends the definition of most authorities as an assessment centre or even a development centre. The essential core of the ACM is the use of some situationally-based exercises to which interviews and tests can be added, if desired, and trained observers and assessors working to predetermined criteria which form the basis of the programme of exercises.

One change, which is related to a change in society in many countries of Europe, is the transfer of greater responsibility to the employees coupled with a greater say in the development of their own careers. This implies a change for ACM, whereby it no longer acts as a vehicle for implementing a centralized career policy, but rather offers the employee an opportunity to gain a personal insight into how he or she performs, and so develop a career from there. This change has taken place in the midst of a growing recognition that companies can no longer project ahead reliably to have a picture of future requirements and opportunities, and that individuals need to do their own predictions, positioning themselves to be well equipped to face whatever develops.

Developments in the assessment centre method

Assessor time

One of the most important factors that an organizer of an assessment centre has to manage is the economic use of the time of assessors and role-players. Increased pressure in business and reduced numbers in the hierarchies have combined to make this a vital issue, limiting the length of an assessment centre and the frequency at which it can be held. There are some methods being tried to find ways of restricting the time demands without appreciably reducing the quality of assessment and development.

The first alternative for limiting the time demands is the use of audio-visual material, such as video. The candidate is presented with open-ended, realistic situations on video. A typical situation may be, for example, that a customer comes to the counter of a travel agent's with a complaint about a holiday just experienced. The conversation is interrupted at a given moment and the candidate is given a number of possible reactions to choose from (detailed descriptions of possible forms of behaviour in the situation). This method allows one or even several role-players to be eliminated per candidate—role-players, indeed, who have to be trained, while a video tape can be copied *ad infinitum* and sent anywhere in the world. Furthermore, video offers a level of standardization that is practically impossible with role-players.

The advantage of this method brings with it, however, a major methodological drawback: in recording the candidate's choice of reaction we are a long way away from assessing behaviour. The candidate says what he or she *would do*, whereas the distinction between what someone says they will do in a given situation and what they actually do is an essential characteristic of the assessment centre method.

The use of video in this way can prove beneficial as a tool for pre-selection when a large number of candidates have to be screened for a particular post, or as a tool for development, because knowing what is the effective behaviour in a given situation is the first step towards exhibiting this behaviour. We also believe that the principle is in itself valuable, in particular with the improvement in standardization, but finding an application that conforms to the requirements of ACM means facilitating interaction with the candidate, which will remain impossible, in our opinion, until developments in the field of visual reality render the method affordable.

Another alternative for limiting the time of assessor involvement is to replace individual role plays with group exercises where each person has a defined role and is required to sustain it. The disadvantage is that the behaviour of the group may be uneven or unrepresentative and may not give each individual a standardized situation, but, as we said above, if more than one actor is used in an individual role-play for various candidates there will not be complete standardization anyway. By varying the composition of groups if there is more than one group exercise it should be possible to see each individual in more than one context to give better reliability.

One trend which may be increasing is for companies to use consultants as assessors, mixed in with company managers. This goes against the principle of ensuring that the 'customers' for the candidates' services are the assessors, but having a proportion of the assessors from outside seems to be acceptable. Indeed, there can be advantages in giving some kind of guarantee that the process conforms to a wider set of standards beyond one company's practices. The cost may be increased, but this may be acceptable if managers are in short supply. Role-players can certainly come from outside the company without any major disadvantage, provided they are capable of sustaining the required role and are well trained.

Use of computers

The most complete application of this development is in the conducting of all tests and exercises by computer, including all role-playing and instructions. Even the candidates' reactions can be processed on the computer, leading to a final assessment. At first sight this method seems a little too technical, but there are in fact a number of good applications. We should point out, however, that this type of application is only justifiable for certain simulations (in-tray, management game, etc.) and with a limited number of criteria (such as problem solving, delegation, etc.). One disadvantage here that should never be underestimated is the fact that only a purely quantitative assessment seems possible, based on results (such as the time needed to analyse data) or a multiple-choice exercise ('To which of the following four people should I delegate this task?'). The computer is incapable of interpreting qualitative data. Moreover, the question arises as to whether applications such as these are acceptable and realistic for the candidate, or, in other words, whether they enjoy the same (high) 'face-validity' as classic assessment centre simulations.

Another application of computers is limited to the processing of results with the use of support software. In such cases the assessment centre is usually operated in the traditional manner, with role-players and assessors writing up in detail all the behavioural nuances of the candidates and providing reports on each candidate for each simulation and each criterion. Only the evaluation discussion looks a little different. The assessors assemble their scores for each candidate, simulation and criterion and enter the data into the computer. The computer then reaches a final score per criterion with the help of a decision model.

Seasoned assessors may view this intervention via the computer as a dilution of the assessment centre's results, but this is not so. Research has shown (Philip Vervaecke, 1993) that the arithmetical average of the criteria scores gives a qualitatively better (more accurate) score than that gained from the evaluation discussion. And an even better method would seem to be that used under the 'expert system' model, whereby a simulation is made of the assessors' ideal decision-making process.

One example of support software being used to process the results of an assessment centre is the decision model adopted by the Dutch bureau Optimum. Once all the assessors have given a score per candidate and per criterion all these scores are entered into the computer. A print-out for a person in an actual case is shown in Figure 6.2.

Mrs. C.H.J.M. VAN DER L
NUMBER 1

	A B C D E F G H I J	AVG	STD	WF	CF
Oral communication	3 3	3.0	0.0	30.0	0
Impact	3 3	3.0	0.0	30.0	0
Initiative	4 3	3.5	0.5	35.0	0
Decisiveness	4 4	4.0	0.0	40.0	0
Flexibility	4 4	4.0	0.0	40.0	0
Sensitivity	4 3	3.5	0.5	35.0	0
Persuasiveness	3 2 2	2.3	0.5	23.3	0
Organizing ability	4 3	3.5	0.5	35.0	0
Judgement	4 2	3.0	1.0	30.0	0
Written communication	4 2	3.0	1.0	30.0	0
		9.0			
		9.0			
		9.0			
		2.3	1.0		0

XX
Salesman to specialist
28/02/1994   Total: 328.3
Simulationday
number 0

Figure 6.2 *Scores of a candidate as entered into computer*

First, the computer calculates an average score per criterion (AVG) and then a total score, with account taken of the weight attached to the criterion concerned. The computer also indicates the extent to which the scores in the various exercises (and thus from the various assessors) deviate from each other (STD). On the basis of this information the figures can be corrected after an evaluation discussion. Following this, a total score is given per candidate (the sum of the weighted criteria scores) and the computer gives a report of how closely the candidate matches the desired profile, as shown in Figure 6.3.

Another software application is where the criteria are weighted according to their importance for different job profiles. One of the consequences is that the assessment centre can, if the necessary validation work has been done, give an indication of the direction in which a career should be developed. A computer can readily be programmed to apply the weightings in these various ways. Not only does this enable the calculations to be done at much greater speed than by other methods, but it has been found to be more reliable and less prone to errors than in calculating in other ways. If there are, for instance, 12 abilities being assessed and some are more important than others, then there could be several factors applied to the scores according to the relative importance of each ability for each relevant job path. This enables total scores to be obtained which can be compared with the norms built up for various careers.

XX   = CLIENT

SALESMAN TO SPECIALISTS   = POSITION

28/02/1994   = DATE

SIMULATIONDAY   = TYPE

0   = NUMBER

APPLICANT	RESULT	SCORE
Mrs. C.H.J.M. V	doesn't come up to the standards	328.3
M.L.A. C	discuss this candidate	410.0
M.M.R.P. R	doesn't come up to the standards	388.3
M.G.M.L. C	doesn't come up to the standards	258.3

Figure 6.3 *List of results and computer report*

The scores and statistics arising from assessment are not necessarily the most important output—the descriptive detail, the individual abilities and ideas for development are often just as important, if not more so—but such figures can give a useful background and provide a stimulus for decisions on career development. Accuracy and reasonable speed in calculation can assist a decision-making group in their evaluation of performance in an assessment centre. Computers that have been pre-programmed to deal with the scores that are agreed by the group can provide a useful service. The implications of the analysis can be looked at by the group while they are in session and are focused on the assessment material.

One use of this is in an organization that offers opportunities for progression to both general management roles and more specialist roles. Some of the abilities are needed in both roles, but often to different extents. And there are one or two abilities which only feature in one of the career paths, which can be represented in the computer program by giving zero weighting against such abilities in career paths where they are not needed.

Table 6.1 illustrates how this can work where there are two career paths involved.

Although some important abilities are shared between the two career paths (such as A and B) this is not always the case (for example, C and E). A weighting system like this is obtained by asking senior managers in both career areas to rank order the abilities and comment on their relevance, after an initial role (or career) analysis has been undertaken. · In this case there may be need for correction of the weighted rating total for Career Path Y by a factor of 17/15 if the total is to be compared with the total for Career Path X. The support of computers can make such matching processes available instantaneously.

Early identification for development

Although assessment centres have frequently been used to identify some people for special forms of development, it is becoming clear that more radical intervention may be needed for some purposes. One example is the building up of a 'cadre' or 'squad' of future international managers who are ready and prepared to move to other countries. An opportunity for development is missed if people are left in their home country for the early part of their career until they have become senior enough to be noticed and are then suddenly asked to move to another country.

Early assessment and discussion for those who might want to become future 'Euromanagers' or international specialists enable plans to be made for career development and early international experience which will make them more effective later. In Chapter 8 we report on a study of criteria for Euromanagers which was aimed at providing ideas for this kind of programme. Some of the other factors which we have found to be relevant are:

Table 6.1   *Differential weighting for asessment for two career paths*

Abilities	Weighting for career path X	Weighting for career path Y
A	3	5
B	4	3
C	4	0
D	2	2
E	0	3
F	2	1
G	1	1
H	1	0
Total	**17**	**15**

- making the Euromanager option explicit at initial selection, e.g. graduate recruitment
- recruiting people from other countries to join a management trainee squad
- having a Euro-squad that is given facilities for 'networking' on a regular basis between countries
- giving extra rewards for language acquisition
- encouraging exchanges, including job exchanges, between countries at various levels in the organization.

Feedback during the assessment centre

In conjunction with the trend towards the use of the term 'development centre' some companies have given the opportunity for assessors and participants to meet after exercises to discuss the events and the behaviour seen. The main purpose of this is to provide a means of learning from the event while it is still fresh in the mind, but it also has the effect of reinforcing the message that the centre has a developmental purpose and that the participant can start taking action on this without waiting until the programme has finished. Each person can thus build up his or her own file on development needs and proposed initiatives. Commitment to the learning opportunities is likely to develop more naturally and more willingly. Some of the reported advantages are:

- earlier development of the relationship between assessor and participant

- development planning can begin while participants and assessors are together in a 'learning community'
- assessors have the opportunity to ask participants why they behaved as they did and what they felt about it
- participants feel more responsibility for the way the event progresses and the outcome from it.

On the other hand, there are some disadvantages:

- the event itself is likely to last longer and cost more in accommodation costs and staff time
- the performance on the measured criteria may change during the event as a result of feedback, thus making it difficult to give a precise picture of development needs
- some participants may take part in exercises in a different order from others, gaining feedback which may change the capabilities shown in other exercises
- there may be confusion about whether it is intended to be a development programme or an assessment of future capabilities and the need for development.

Whether or not to use this change of method is a decision that should be determined by the defined purpose of the event.

Group assessment

A possible and probably necessary development of the ACM is the introduction of centres for the assessment and development of groups. The intention is not actually to assess how a given individual behaves in a group—a conventional AC can do this if the criteria and exercises are designed for this. What concerns us here is the evolution and functioning of self-managing work teams and other new forms of co-operation that are currently becoming popular in the business world. The behaviour of a group, rather than an individual, is obviously more complex to assess with the emphasis on performance of the group as a whole.

The whole domain of 'team building' is involved and, although there are a number of training programmes designed for this, the reasons and objectives are usually less clear than for individual training programmes. The starting point is to define 'group performance criteria' and then design exercises that relate to these in the context in which the group has to work. Assessing group behaviour in a systematic and consistent way is still in its early stages. However, progress has already been made in designing exercises for assessing the 'managers' (or 'facilitators') of self-managing work teams.

Assessment in a 'flattened' organization

The changes that have taken place in companies in a number of countries in Europe in the early nineties have involved the removal of some layers of management so that there are fewer levels between operating staff and top management. Assessment centres were developed under conditions of ample levels of middle management from which a ready supply of assessors could be obtained. The removal of several levels implies a reduction in the number of supervising managers, and those that are left are responsible for larger groups of people with consequently less time available for extra activities such as assessment centres. There is also a greater risk that an individual will have to be observed in an assessment centre by someone who is the immediate manager of that individual, which offends a normal principle of ACM.

Another difficulty of using assessment centres in a flatter organization is that there are fewer opportunities for 'upward' progression. Individuals who invest time and energy in an assessment/development centre often have an explicit or implicit expectation that some form of promotion could result from it, sooner or later. Those operating ACM need to make clear to participants that the outcome and consequent development plans are primarily geared towards identifying improvements in performance without movement up the hierarchy.

Ownership of assessment data

In the early applications of ACM, for instance with AT&T in the USA in the sixties, it was assumed that the employer owned the information that was collected and could use it, or not use it, for managerial purposes without giving any right of decision about this to the candidate. As the method became more widely used and the protection of personal data became an issue in society in many countries, questions began to be asked about the use of data and the respecting of confidentiality with regard to personal data. In Europe it is now becoming agreed that it is, in the first place, the assessee who should decide what happens to the information, even if the company pays the cost of the assessment centre and offers the opportunity to participate. Although there is some pressure on the individual to agree to making the results available to selected members of management it is becoming accepted he or she should not be forced to do so.

In Dutch companies there are often arrangements that the results should not be kept in the company files for longer than a certain limited period as people change and develop continuously. The French concept of 'Balance of Skills' is an excellent idea: one can work on improving one's ability and, after a year has passed, a new 'Balance' is formulated.

Self-assessment and self-development

A number of influences are pointing towards a more radical development in ACM, although some experiments have been in operation for about 10 years. This is for an organization to provide an opportunity for people to review their options and devise their own development plans with expert assistance. For participants to be in a position where they can reliably assess themselves and other participants in this event they need to be given training as assessors and feedback counsellors. It is likely that this will double the time taken in the group event, but to balance this there will be less requirement for other staff to serve as assessors and less need after the event to have feedback sessions and other management involvement.

Two members of Assessment Circle Europe cooperated in 1984 in running such an event for 12 people, where the participants had to do all the observing for each other and, in small groups of four people, built up an assessment picture for each other and then used the resources of the full group to set objectives and move into development. In 1985 Hoechst (UK) started running development centres which used self- and peer assessment for a large proportion of the work of the event (Griffiths and Allen, 1987). In 1994 we are working with clients who, because they are reducing the number of hierarchical layers in the organization, are dispensing with line manager assessors. One benefit of this change is that it will normally satisfy the condition of confidentiality of data, stressed earlier. Having been helped to produce the data in conditions of self- and peer assessment it is then natural to assume that the individual owns the results and can decide whether or not to share them with those who are in managerial roles in relation to the individual.

A parallel development is for government agencies, as is happening in France, to provide facilities for individuals to be assessed externally, and to be helped to devise a development plan outside their employment. With changing technologies and business methods it may become normal for most people to undertake such a review every five years or so to ensure that their employability remains at a satisfactory level.

Summary

In this chapter we have suggested ways in which managers and human resource specialists who want to plan strategically to provide assessment and development systems which will match the future environment may need to apply their efforts. The following questions may help to summarize the ideas:

- Are assessment and development methods based on an analysis of current and future job and career demands?
- If the assessment centre method is used, is it being used to its full potential of stimulating development and providing clear behavioural criteria for appraisal purposes?
- Is it necessary to reduce the time demands on line managers by use of video, computers, actors or consultants, or by redesigning the assessment or development method?
- Is there a need to identify some forms of potential very early in order to intervene with special development programmes?
- Are there self-directed work teams which might benefit from group assessment so that they can be helped to develop faster as high-performing teams?
- Has the 'flattened' organization been taken fully into account in

ensuring that assessment, appraisal and development systems match this new situation?

● Is it clear who owns any assessment data and that such information is able to be used by individuals as fully as possible in developing their performance and careers?

References   Fombrun, C., Tichy, N.M. and Devanna, M.A. (eds) (1984) *Strategic Human Resource Management*, John Wiley, New York.

Griffiths, P. and Allen, B. (1987) 'Assessment Centres: Breaking with Tradition', *Journal of Management Development*, Vol. 6, No. 1.

Huck, J.R. (1973) 'Assessment Centers: a review of the internal and external validities', *Personnel Psychology*, Vol. 26, No. 2.

Megginson, D. and Pedler, M. (1992) *Self-development: a facilitator's guide*, McGraw-Hill, Maidenhead.

Schuler, H. and Stehle, W. (Hrsg.) (1987) *Assessment center als Methods der Personalentwicklung*, Verlag für augewaudte Psychologie, Stuttgart.

Vervaecke, P. (1993) 'Actuele stand van de evaluatie de psychometrische kwaliteiten van de Assessment Center Method', presentation at the second Belgian congress on the Assessment Centre Method.

Werkgroep Assessment Centers Vlaanderen (1992) 'Richtlijnen en ethische overwegingen bij het toepassen van de Assessment Center Methode', Vocap, Belgium.

7 Language and cultural adaptation

Ulrike Hess

The following report describes experiences with two projects where 'tpm' of Germany developed assessment centres for other countries. It is not intended to give detailed descriptions of the two projects, but merely a few highlights that might be typical for this kind of transfer.

Both projects were for companies manufacturing motor cars. The two countries in which these assessment centres were held were Turkey and Hungary. Common to both projects is that at the time of the projects both countries had very limited experience with selection procedures like these. This makes it even more interesting to compare these two countries with each other.

Assessment centres for Turkey

Starting point

Initially the responsible manager from the German company asked tpm whether it would be prepared to select employees for a new motor car plant to be erected in Izmir, Turkey. The method to be applied for the selection was that of assessment centres (the company had always applied this method in the past. Employees for three hierarchical levels had to be selected, namely chief engineers (reporting to the production manager), team leaders and team members. Only the German production manager and the Turkish managers responsible for maintenance, materials and planning had already been appointed in Turkey at that point.

In cooperation with these managers we first selected the chief engineers with this method. The chief engineers then became the new observers and assessors for the selection of team leaders, who in turn selected the team members.

While selection took place the factory was built and equipped.

Description of the assessment centres

During the development of the assessment centre we took care that the criteria, according to which the participants were to be assessed, fulfilled the philosophy of the company. This was ensured by interviewing responsible employees of the company in Germany and Turkey.

The criteria also had to be compatible with all three hierarchical levels, since certain requirements were demanded from *all* employees independent of their future work (e.g. teamwork, initiative, critical thinking).

The exercises of the assessment centre, however, clearly differed for the various levels.

For the highest level mainly management tasks (such as team meetings, negotiations, team-leading exercises, in-tray exercises) were planned. Technical exercises tailored to future work situations were part of the team leader assessment. For example, car doors and windows had to be installed, dented parts had to be panelbeaten and spray-painted and electric fittings had to be installed during these exercises.

The procedure for the team members was split up into technical exercises and exercises for the observation of social and methodical abilities as well as for the assessment of personal competence, e.g. perseverance.

First, the technical abilities of the applicants were evaluated by local instructors. The assessment centre then followed, with the assistance of tpm.

In total 170 employees were selected in this way. Since the production plant is continuously expanding, new employees constantly have to be selected. In the meantime the responsible people have acquired the know-how of the procedure and only require tpm's supervision. They run the assessment centres themselves.

Acceptance of the procedures

These assessment centres were probably the first ever to be held in Turkey. Therefore it was exciting to see how such a procedure would be accepted by the Turkish people.

In all aspects we were pleasantly surprised: right from the beginning to the end of the project everyone concerned was most willing to ensure the exact and competent organization and implementation of the assessment centres. We were also surprised by the willingness of the participants to take part in a procedure unfamiliar to them.

The first assessment centre selecting engineers had to be held in rented offices in Izmir. The furnishing of these rooms obviously had to be rearranged for this purpose.

A whole technical college was then rented and equipped for the team leader assessment centre. This event especially had a highly complex schedule—it had to cater for 45 participants and 20 observers in various task groups for the assessment in different group compositions and with various exercise sequences. Thanks to the high degree of discipline and the distinct organizational talent of everyone involved, hardly anything went wrong.

Owing to technical reasons the first few assessment centres took place at weekends. It was remarkable that all applicants who were invited took part in the assessment centre and all those participating on Saturdays came back on Sundays. Because of the tight time schedule the observers were under even greater stress, since they had to evaluate the day's performances in the evenings, but they also fulfilled their task meticulously and concentrated at a high level right through to the end of the project. Moreover, both participants and observers enjoyed taking part in the assessment centres.

It was certainly an advantage that the company was a well-known employer and therefore attracted many qualified applicants, and that the excellent products and working conditions to be expected in a new factory were appealing, attractive and motivating.

Language problems Initially the assessment centre was developed and drawn up by tpm in German. The Turkish translator was involved in the work right from the beginning to obtain an understanding of the procedure in order to translate the contents of the assessment centre satisfactorily into Turkish.

The procedure itself was multilingual. For the levels of chief engineers and team leaders, only applicants with a knowledge of either English or German were invited. Here we found that most Turks had an excellent knowledge of English. During the assessment centre the instructions for observers and participants were in German or English, the exercises in the participants' native language, Turkish. The evaluation of the results was again carried out in English and German, which meant that the Turkish observers had to translate the results and their observations at once. All in all, it was a lengthy and exhausting procedure, but it led to a good result with everyone being highly motivated.

Organization One problem which we underestimated at the time of planning was the transport of the material from the tpm offices to Izmir. Since only a small office in Turkey was available at the beginning, it was necessary to compile all the material for the assessment centre in Germany (documents, observers' files, material for the exercises, etc.).

Nine big metal suitcases therefore had to be air-freighted for the first assessment centre. Some of them were promptly confiscated at Customs. However, thanks to the improvization and skill of the Turkish partners the material was released after a few hours and guaranteed a good start of the assessment centre.

Another problem for the organization of the procedure was the poor telephone communications between Turkey and Germany at that time; these have improved greatly since then.

Cultural adaptation   Implementing an assessment centre in another country requires adaptation of the exercises and criteria to that country. We therefore carried out various interviews with Turkish people and responsible employees of the company. This ensured that every exercise and task could be coped with by the applicants and that it offered a challenge to them.

The same applied for the criteria. Not every criterion—even if it is well translated—has the same meaning in every country. An example of this is the term 'leadership'. In Germany this expression mainly stands for cooperative leadership behaviour such as delegating, giving feedback, giving a word of praise or criticism, motivating, controlling, etc. In Turkey leadership means authority as well. Authority is inevitable for a Turkish manager if he or she wants to be accepted in his or her position. Therefore this term is best described by: acting in agreement with the hierarchy, behaving as a person in authority, keeping a distance from other levels without appearing arrogant, setting an example to others, keeping calm and collected.

The difference in the understanding of the manager's role as described above shows that a sound knowledge and comprehension of the country's culture is necessary before being able to work as a consultant in that country and to assess applicants as to whether or not they are suitable for specific jobs.

Apart from the questions regarding the contents of the assessment centre the German consultants also had to inform themselves about customs in Turkey, e.g. expressing invitations, giving presents, behaviour of males and females, etc. Extremely valuable was the help of an employee of tpm who had been brought up in Turkey and could be consulted during the whole project. She gave us important information and tips in this respect.

Assessment centres for Hungary

When comparing the development and implementation of the assessment centres for Hungary with those in Turkey, almost no differences in principle can be found between the two projects.

The company involved was the same as in Turkey. The project was a joint venture with a Hungarian truck manufacturer as partner. Team leaders had to be selected for the factory in Hungary.

The emphasis of this assessment centre was put on manual exercises. These had to be done in groups of two or more participants, and certain tools had to be assembled according to written instructions. We were especially interested to assess the leadership behaviour of each participant. For this purpose one participant always had to take over, in turn, the role of a team leader in these exercises.

In another exercise, the participants had to solve a written situation and planning task in groups of two. A mechanical-technical comprehension test and individual interviews were also held.

Again in Hungary we experienced that everyone involved with the procedure was willing to help with the organization, to remove any stumbling blocks and to provide the best possible working conditions for their guests from West Germany. The reason for their courtesy was probably the fact that at that time (1989) Hungary was already orientating itself towards Western countries.

Language problems   The language issue in Hungary was solved as follows. All documents for the assessment centre were translated into Hungarian. During the assessment centre each group of observers had their own Hungarian translator for every exercise. This translator not only read the instructions to the participants, but also translated certain passages during the exercises, as well as important statements made by participants, to the observers in a low voice. The (English and German) observers made their notes in English or German . The evaluation was held in English. Since the participants did manual work in many exercises, their gestures and facial expressions were also indications to the observers during assessment: an interesting experience for everyone.

Conclusions and limitations

Our experience, of which we have reported only two cases, shows that the assessment centre method can be transferred to other countries without major problems, even if there are language changes, provided certain intentions can be transferred:

- that the assessment centre is a fair procedure in which assessments and decisions taken are comprehensible to all participants
- that it has been set up as a valid procedure which makes demands on the participants which reflect the future work situation.

On the other hand, the assessment centre also has a few limitations in its application, for example in countries (such as Arab countries) where it is beneath someone's dignity to be observed during work. Also, cultures which do not offer the prerequisite of 'equal rights for all' are not suitable for the implementation of this method.

A thorough analysis of the cultural circumstances is therefore always the first step to be taken before this method can be applied in a foreign country. It then depends on the sensitivity and creativity of the consultant to recommend and develop suitable procedures, using the help of those who know the language and culture from the inside.

8 The ability to work and learn together across Europe

Ulrike Hess, Mac Bolton, Victor Ernoult, Jan Gijswijt, Hélio Moreira and Lou Van Beirendonck

In this final chapter we try to be futuristic and report on our studies of what managers and their cooperation can be if we take the trouble to plan ahead and are sensitive in our working together across boundaries of nations and cultures.

In the first part of the chapter, we report the results of a study we carried out to try to establish criteria for selecting and developing the 'Euromanagers' of the future. This does not claim to give a final definitive answer, but the material produced came from in-depth interviews with experienced managers from five countries which also drew from those managers' experience in other countries.

In the second part, we report on an attempt by five of the authors to be honest about their own experiences in working together within the Assessment Circle Europe group itself. In other words, we put the spotlight on ourselves and are prepared to be honest about the difficulties and rewards from five years of working and learning together as a group of organizational psychologists involved in business. The information came from taking part in a seminar at the 17th Congress for Applied Psychology of the German Psychology Society held in Bonn in September 1993. Being honest about your relationships with colleagues from other countries, in front of an audience of about 40 mainly German psychologists, was an interesting experience. The audience seemed to receive it enthusiastically, and perhaps this way of discussing it could be a model for learning about international relationships.

Characteristics of successful 'Euro-managers': results of a study by occupational and organizational psychologists from five European countries

Objective The ACE group (Assessment Circle Europe) intended to hold a workshop on 'Assessing and Developing Managers for Cross-national Working' in October 1992. In preparation for the workshop, ACE planned to develop an assessment centre for assessing the potential of future 'cross-culture' managers. Part of the development involved the definition of criteria that can be applied for successful appointments of managers in foreign countries. These criteria were intended to serve the participants of the workshop as a basis for discussions and structuring the work to test and develop assessment centre exercises together.

Method

Data research Between March and May 1992 ACE members held 11 interviews with personnel experts who have experience in selecting, developing and taking care of employees working in a foreign country.

The various topics and questions which were to be addressed during the interviews were summarized into the following guidelines:

1 Giving an outline of ACE and the objective of the workshop (aim of the workshop: to find better means of assessment of employees for cross-cultural working).
2 Job description of the interviewee.
3 Criteria for successful cross-cultural managers

- Which know-how and abilities should a cross-cultural manager have?
- Are there typical careers?
- Which obstacles are present in cross-cultural working, i.e. what reasons are mentioned for not being placed abroad?

4 What can be said for or against foreign appointments?

- Are some study directions more suitable than others for a transfer abroad?
- What are the reasons for unsuccessful foreign appointments?

5 A description of one case where cross-cultural working was successful and one where it was not.

Evaluation The records of the interviews that were written up either in English or German were evaluated quantitatively. Main statements made during the interviews were systematized by means of the 'metaplan' technique which clustered them, allotting them to main topics. The various statements under each topic were further subdivided into main criteria and subsidiary ones. Each statement made was taken into account even if it was mentioned more than once. Furthermore, each statement was regarded as equally important without quantitative or weighted evaluation.

The criteria that are derived should be seen as the result of a provisional exploration and as an approach to the subject. They are intended as an aid for further discussion and for further development of assessment criteria as needed for cross-cultural managers. The advantage of these reported results lies in the fact that experts from different nationalities were interviewed and therefore impressions of various European perspectives were obtained.

Results   The evaluation of the interviews came up with five relevant subjects which are of importance for planned cross-cultural working:

1 Preparation phase
2 Social integration/construction of social network
3 Personal prerequisites
4 Existing abilities and those to be developed
5 Re-integration.

Preparation phase   • support by the company
• individual's activities.

Important for successful foreign appointments is the intensive and sufficient preparation of the employee for his or her planned transfer. Not only language courses, seminars and training are necessary, but also social and organizational preparation such as introductions to relevant contacts and finding suitable accommodation. The family should already be involved at this stage. It is important that the employee is offered sufficient support and possibilities by the company. Equally important is the initiative and activity from the employee to prepare him or herself mentally for the new environment and to come to terms with the conditions and challenges awaiting him or her.

Social integration/   • support by the company
construction of social   • individual's activities
network   • recommendations.

According to the experience which the interviewees had had, a successful social integration is important. In particular, the integration of the family is a factor for success that is not to be underestimated. This applies not only for the settling-in phase but also for the duration of the stay abroad. Integration is influenced by the living environment and social contacts. Continuation of social and financial security overseas as well as in the native country must be guaranteed. Support both by the company and by the employee's own and his or her family's activities are required. British and German interviewees especially emphasized the importance of the preparation phase and social integration.

Personal prerequisites [The letters in brackets after the statements listed below indicate the nationality of the interviewee who gave the statement: i.e. D = Germany, E = Great Britain, F = France, H = The Netherlands, P = Portugal.]

- knowledge of language

  —perfect knowledge of foreign language (D)
  —sound knowledge of the country's language, even if the 'company language' is English (E)
  —knowledge of languages: especially English (F)
  —language abilities (F)

- international experience

  —having international experience or being raised in an internationally orientated environment (D)
  —international orientation (E)
  —international experience—makes it easier for a renewed process of adaptation (F)

- job experience/qualification

  —4–5 years' job experience at head office (D)
  —experience of personnel responsibilities (D)
  —having experience at work in dealing with people (D)
  —acknowledged and visible know-how (E)
  —good experience in the working field that is locally important (F)
  —technical abilities (F)

- intrinsic motivation

  —employee has to recognize the need for moving abroad (D)
  —combining personal motives with being in a foreign country (D)
  —willing to deal with foreign culture (D)
  —having perspectives for the period following his or her stay abroad (D)
  —willing to increase international communication (F)
  —high motivation to discover new cultures and new techniques (F)
  —being able to use the international experience gained after his or her return (F)
  —being motivated to move abroad (P)

- mobility

  —favourable requirements for high mobility: under 40 or over 50 in age and no family ties or house ownership (D)

—willing to travel (F)
—geographical mobility (F)

The prerequisites mentioned above relate to the necessary qualifications and the motivation of future cross-cultural managers. A pre-selection will show to what extent these prerequisites are fulfilled. The know-how and competence gained by job experience and the affiliation with headquarters are of importance here. Another criterion is an appropriate knowledge of the language. This can be learned and improved during preparation time. It is advantageous if the employee has international experience or shows an international orientation. Furthermore, the intrinsic motivation of the employee, i.e. his or her interest in foreign cultures, working conditions and tasks as well as mobility, are deciding factors.

Existing abilities and those to be developed

General basic abilities

- initiative and activity, 'to get something in motion'

    —developing high activity and initiative (D)
    —activity; ability to be active and not only administrative; ability to set up systems and use them as such; ability to organize (F)
    —taking initiative; entrepreneurial abilities; being creative; to improvise; trying to find solutions; making suggestions (H)

- independent acting

    —not to expect specific work instructions, but rather finding them on one's own (D)
    —ability to establish one's own information network (F)
    —being able to cope without the support of relatives and family; being autonomous and imaginative (P)

- goal-orientated acting

    —getting on with the job rather than exploring blind alleys (E)
    —strong convictions; being able to say 'no'; determination; ability to keep to objectives and goals and to set new perspectives; scientific attitude but pragmatic attitude first (F)
    —productivity; being a winner; getting results; getting to the essence, to the centre of problems (H)
    —doing whatever is needed to obtain results; ability to define goals and tasks (P)

- cognitive and planning abilities, network thinking

    —thinking systematically (D)
    —being able to handle unexpected results; being aware of problems, willing to find solutions and be aware of possible difficulties, not

to underestimate problems; being able to distinguish between urgencies and priorities; to keep in mind the objectives; to keep an eye on everything; general overview (F)

—anticipating, foreseeing consequences; taking into consideration possible reactions and formulating answers in advance (H)

—being competent in planning and controlling with different types of resources (P)

- mental and physical ability to cope with stress

—ability to cope with stress and show endurance (D)

—flexibility regarding travelling and working hours (E)

—ability to cope with several problems at the same time (F)

—being able to work in stress situations (H)

—resistance to frustration and stress, when not obtaining things in the accustomed way (P)

- communication and interpersonal skills

—contact with groups outside the company; ability to lead others; being extrovert (D)

—sociable; to listen and to discuss differing views on a one-to-one basis, not to get involved in intrigues; to be good with contacts and networks; passing on one's know-how to other experts; being able to communicate with colleagues of all levels (E)

—leadership ability; ability to influence; willingness to develop local employees; ability to convince; communication abilities; communications skills; ability to listen; able to communicate own results; to spend time with one's first line managers (F)

—listening skills together with radiating trustworthiness; being able to work in a team (H)

Adjustment and integration into the new culture

- Maintaining the balance between own and foreign culture

—awareness of one's own cultural background; representative of own country; keeping one's personality; not giving up one's cultural identity; communication with head office; keeping up-to-date with changes at head office (D)

—being open-minded to other cultures without giving up one's own culture (E)

—ability to move within both cultures; being aware of own culture; ability to find one common language (official language must be the language of the mother company); no complete identification with the local work and lifestyle (F)

- respect for different opinions, values, etc.

—no prejudice (D)

—no prejudice regarding the culture; accepting the other culture and building thereon, instead of imposing one's own ideas onto others;

accepting and building on the existing, rather than imposing one's own principles; being able to appraise oneself, accepting one's own values, etc. and those of others (E)

—tolerance, respect for others; being aware of the relativity of own values; ability to doubt oneself; respect for the local culture; respecting different strategies in finding solutions to problems and different working habits (F)

—being able to exclude own prejudices, preferences and hobbies from chosen solutions and viewpoints (H)

- finding compromises, willingness to compromise

—finding central solutions; able to meet people half-way (E)

—ability to find consensus with the partners; limiting an academic approach to management/not trying to enforce systems without trying to adapt; being able to adapt to local procedures, even if they are shocking; being sensitive to local differences and willing to integrate them; able to keep high standards (F)

—being flexible and not trying to impose one's own point of view onto others; by having the company policies and procedures in mind, to adjust them to the needs and resources available locally without just following the original ones; ability to adapt to situations with fewer resources and different working conditions (P)

- being open-minded and willing to learn

—open to foreign culture (D)

—ability to understand the local situation, to know what is good there and add it to one's own set of values; being open and willing to learn, recognizing that there will be some elements of best practice to be found wherever you go; being open-minded and willing to adapt to the new manager and the new culture; ability to 'plug into' experts, willing to seek advice (E)

—being open-minded to local way of working rather than being too convinced of the accustomed style; ability to learn diverse jobs; high intellectual level, mental openness; open to the environment; open to the local conditions (F)

- social and cultural sensibility

—appropriate manner; quickly assessing the order of ranking (D)

—to understand and to have some empathy with the local culture; being aware of the advantage of being different (in national origin) (E)

—having a good perception of needs (F)

—showing awareness of different feelings, opinions and preferences in others; having a good sense of nuances; balanced judgements; having opinions which have been well reflected on and making careful judgements based on facts; making distinction between facts and feelings; being aware of the relativity of certain facts and aspects (H).

The abilities and potentials listed above are the actual criteria which can be applied during assessment of personnel, e.g. during an assessment centre. These are basic abilities referring to the motivational, cognitive and social requirements that cross-cultural managers should fulfil. Furthermore, the criteria include specific abilities and requirements important for successful adaptation and integration into a foreign culture. These could provide the focus for individual or group development plans for people planning to move into cross-cultural working.

Re-integration   Another topic, which was mentioned by only some people interviewed, refers to the evaluation after returning from abroad, the re-integration in the country of origin and the benefit of the experience gained. The ACE members agreed that the 'coming home' phase in particular is often neglected and more importance should be given to it during the planning phase.

Further information should be gathered on this subject. It should be examined whether the evaluation afterwards and the re-integration influence the entire benefit of cross-cultural appointments and what supporting and accompanying measures would be useful.

Conclusions and discussion   When the results of our research are compared with others, similar criteria are mentioned but they occupy different central positions. It is mostly the technical prerequisites of cross-cultural managers that are looked at. Only then—if at all—is there mention of the criteria related to the personality, or the attitude of the spouse or family towards a stay in a foreign country (Pausenberger and Noelle, 1977, page 350 ff; Steinmann and Kumar, 1976, page 84; Ronen, 1986, page 533).

Available literature on results of studies, however, show criteria that are very similar to ours. Great importance is attached especially to the criteria 'cultural open-mindedness' and 'family' (Mendenhall, Dunbar and Oddou, 1987, page 333; Rehfuss, 1982, page 35 ff).

The original aim of the ACE group was to develop an assessment centre. To achieve this, it was necessary to define assessment criteria for managers suitable for appointment abroad. Following this, criteria will have to be operationalized so that they can be applied for observation of participants in assessment centre exercises.

In the meantime various assessment centre exercises and tasks which represent situations for cross-cultural managers have been developed. The ACE group has dealt with this part of the project in intercultural cooperation; this ensures that the exercises can be translated with equal success for the different nationalities.

The criteria mentioned can thus serve as a basis for evaluation of potential as well as for the means of specific personnel development. During preparation of seminars existing abilities could be specifically strengthened and trained.

Apart from the technical results of the ACE cooperation, the members gained personal profit from their work together. They have learned and are still learning to make an effort to understand their team partners despite different languages and mentalities, to learn about their motives and interests and to consider these in their work. In the next section we report on our wider experience on several other joint projects over a longer time period.

Reflections on the intercultural cooperation of psychologists from five European countries

We report here our frank reflections on our efforts to work together (as Assessment Circle Europe) in a total group of about 10 psychologists who normally work separately in small organizations in each country. Five of us were able to come together for the occasion of the 17th Congress in Applied Psychology organized by German psychologists in September 1993 in Bonn. Unfortunately our colleagues from France were not able to be with us on that occasion. As part of our presentation in one of the workshops we each tried to answer the questions:

- What experience have I gained from cooperating with psychologists from different European countries in the ACE group?
- What recommendations can I give to other European teams?

The answers to these questions touched very diverse aspects. We have grouped them under headings which have enabled most of the comments to be brought together in an understandable way which could have relevance to wider groups.

Gain of professional know-how

Each ACE member has a different professional development, experience, individual emphasis of interests and cultural background. This was a big advantage for the work in the ACE group, since each member had acquired professional competence in various fields.

The members benefited greatly from the information exchange relating to this knowledge and experience, e.g. 'I can benefit from their experience', 'I get information', '... new ideas, for example the technique called metaplan ...' (Portugal).

Learning new methods and the acquisition of expert knowledge were mentioned: '... the British colleagues are doing a lot of work on the development of criteria ..., the Dutch partners are experts on using computer techniques in assessment centres. The French use a lot of media, for instance, videorecorders ...', (Germany). Reference was also made to gaining a better understanding of the country's economic system by comparison to other systems in other European countries.

The different perspectives of members inspired and contributed to a more comprehensive understanding of questions and problems and to the development of new ideas. Working together creates a network of experiences and makes it possible for many kinds of practical experience to be gathered: 'You have access to information, to events . . .' (Portugal).

All of this, together with international connections resulting from this cooperation, leads to a higher personal and professional credibility which contributes to a greater persuasiveness in one's own work: 'When I feel more confident, I am more action-driven . . .' (Portugal).

Personal experiences

Working in an intercultural team is seen as a challenge and, in addition to the professional gain, a means of learning to know oneself.

The work makes one sensitive to colleagues, helping one to understand others better and promotes flexibility in thinking and acting: 'You have to link ideas and you have got to try to make it work . . .' (Portugal). This leads to more tolerance in many fields: 'Each of us here has some good points to make, we all have a contribution, so we must wait for it, look for it . . .' (Britain).

Speaking a foreign language constantly increases each member's competence in that language. The result is a higher level of self-confidence in the professional and personal field.

Gaining professional know-how in connection with positive personal experience, e.g. finding new friends, is experienced as exciting and personally satisfying.

Establishment of an intercultural group

The development of cooperation in a group like this one progresses only slowly. With ACE this was an evolutionary process over many years. New members joined over the years and it took quite a while until the members became a team.

A common basis, a wealth of common values and a sense that each member contributes something important as well as other mutualities provide the foundation of this growing together. It is supported by a high willingness of all to cooperate by openness and by the will to work together. The engagement and motivation of each to achieve the common goals, and mutual tolerance in the work, marked the development of the group: 'Motivation is the motor, also for cooperation . . .' (Holland).

Although social norms vary, they seldom cause serious misunderstandings. In the process, openness and the intention to achieve a common goal are experienced more intensely than the separating intercultural differences. In this context, it appears that differences between psychological schools are often greater than between different cultures!

Difficulties

There are many possibilities to gain personally and professionally from the intercultural work, but at the same time various problems arise.

Language is the biggest problem of all. (The working language of the group was agreed at one of the first meetings to be English.) The different language levels within the group hinder communication. It leads to misunderstandings and to only partial comprehension, and also to the difficulty in finding words for one's thoughts: 'I am very unhappy when I cannot say what I want to say ...' (Germany).

When a language is not mastered well, great difficulties can occur when complex psychological concepts are intended to be translated without a loss of meaning. This sometimes results in inconsistencies and mistakes which increase the insecurity of some members.

Working in a foreign language is tiring and causes strain, frustration and stress. Creative procedures and considerable additional expenditure of energy and time are needed for achieving mutual understanding: 'You need to put in more effort ...' (Portugal). The integration of different procedures increases the strain even further.

At first, the person working in his or her native home language seems to have an advantage: 'It's less tiring ...' (Britain); but great sensitivity is asked of this person: 'I have to remember colleagues are not working in their own language' (Britain). The person has to hold back and has to be careful not to dominate: 'I can find the word quickly... I could dominate a conversation if I wanted to ...' (Britain). There is also a risk that great strain is put on the British members by assuming that everything that has to be written will be done by them.

Because representatives of diverse cultures are working together, members very politely stay in the background to a certain extent. The result is that nobody wants to take over the leadership: 'We are always very polite to each other, and sometimes I miss not having a leader, someone who says how we should do something ...' (Germany).

An aspect not to be forgotten is the high travelling costs with no immediate financial benefit; but it is exciting and satisfying when the above-mentioned difficulties are overcome and the common goal is achieved: 'To do things interculturally, to feel that we understand each other and are gaining from working with each other is very exciting' (Britain).

Recommendations   The reflections on and discussion of experience gained during the work with ACE has resulted in some recommendations for effective cooperation of intercultural teams within Europe:

1 Fundamental for cooperation is a knowledge of the working language. The better the knowledge, the easier and more effective the work with one another. Therefore people intending to work in an intercultural context are recommended to obtain a knowledge of the required language in good time.
2 Visits to the country concerned are advisable, also to get to know foreign cultures more generally: 'Living in another culture makes it easier to work with a third culture' (Holland).

3 The experience of the starting phase of the ACE group shows that it is advisable for similar projects to establish only a few, but close, contacts with partners from other countries.

4 Generous time planning is imperative for cooperation of this kind: 'Decisions take longer' (Portugal). Actions often take double or triple the time for planning and implementation: 'If you are planning a German meeting and you think two hours are enough, you have to plan three or four hours for a European meeting' (Germany). More time is especially needed until the strength and professional competence of partners is identified.

5 It is also recommended to discuss openly and explicitly the language competence of everybody in advance, so that the group takes the differences into account in their work later on: 'People may be feeling that they are not very competent and they don't want to admit it. I think it is better to discuss it openly' (Britain).

6 Everyone has something to contribute. Therefore it is essential that everyone gets enough time to look for the words for what he or she wants to say: 'Often we had to wait a little to watch for him to catch up and make his point, because he always had some good points to make' (Britain).

7 It is important to adapt to the different thinking and procedures and to accept them, i.e. not to jump to conclusions just because they are different. The respective context is taken into account in each case according to the slogan: 'International perspective—local relevance' (Belgium).

8 It is important to ask questions in order to be sure that a person's remarks are understood correctly. This prevents misunderstandings right from the start: 'You have to get feedback on whether you are understood or not' (Germany).

9 Non-verbal communication has an important function in these groups. A *questioning* facial expression indicates uncertainty. Strain and feeling burdened can also be expressed non-verbally: '. . . true of all intercultural working: to get to know these signals and to be more aware of them' (Britain).

10 Written work should preferably be done by those who are fluent in the language. This is to prevent strain on those less competent in the language, though care should be taken not to overtax the colleague who does this.

11 When difficulties arise, not too much importance should be attached to the differences. The mutualities should rather be constantly kept in mind: 'It could be harder to work with colleagues of other psychological approaches or schools in your own country than to work with psychologists all over Europe' (Britain).

References Mendenhall, M., Dunbar, E. and Oddou, G. (1987) 'Expatriate selection, training and career-pathing: a review and critique', *Human Resource Management*, 26 (3), pp 331–345.

Pausenberger, E. and Noelle, G.F. (1977) 'Entsendung von Führungskräften in ausländische Niederlassungen', *Schmalenbachs Zeitschrift für betriebswirtschaft-liche Forschung*, 29, S.346–366.

Rehfuss, J. (1982) 'Management development and the selection of overseas executives', *Personnel Administrator*, July, pp 35–44.

Ronen, S. (1986) *Comparative and multinational management*, John Wiley, New York.

Steinmann, Horst and Kumar, Brij (1976) 'Angst vor der Rückkehr, Deutsche Manager im Ausland', *Management Magazin*, 12, S.84–92.

Trompenaars, F. (1993) *Riding the Waves of Culture: understanding cultural diversity in business*, The Economist Books, London.

Wirth, E. (1992) *Mitarbeiter im Auslandseinsatz*, Gabler, Wiesbaden.

Index

Further titles in the McGraw-Hill Training Series

All books are published by:

McGraw-Hill Book Company Europe
Shoppenhangers Road, Maidenhead, Berkshire SL6 2QL, England
Tel: (01628) 23432   Fax: (01628) 770224